for Connie Zboray
with all best wishes.

Merle A. Irwin

BIBLE STORIES IN THE FIRST PERSON

by

Merle S. Irwin

A Hearthstone Book

Carlton Press, Inc.   New York, N.Y.

Dedicated
to the seven churches
that inspired one to preach
better than he knew:

First Presbyterian, Britton, South Dakota

New Castle Presbyterian, New Castle, Delaware

The Church Afloat, the USS Rocky Mount in the South Pacific,
World War II

The Presbyterian Church in Westfield, N.J.

First Presbyterian, Poughkeepsie, N.Y.

Bloomfield Presbyterian Church on the Green,
Bloomfield, New Jersey

The Huguenot Memorial Presbyterian Church,
Pelham, New York

Artist:
Scott Irwin Holden
Age 9

ACKNOWLEDGMENTS

to the Rev. Dr. J. Edgar Pearson of the Synod of Washington for launching a fledgling preacher into "First Person" sermons.

to Edlers William and Gladys McGill of the Poughkeepsie Church for printing and circulating the first series of sermons.

to Barbara Irwin Holden for the manuscript and editing, and to Scott Irwin Holden for the art work.

"The history of the world is composed of the biographies of its great men."

So wrote Thomas Carlyle. But more vivid than biographies written by others, are autobiographies.

The Bible is interested in telling the story of God's love as it was revealed to people through the centuries. It is a meeting place where you are forever running into an Infinite Mind and coming upon the yearning of an Eternal Heart.

The Bible is basically a biography of Jesus Christ and not a biography of men and women. Yet the story of those whose lives were touched by the Christ can yet help people in every age to pronounce God's name with power in the arena of life where they live and work and have their being.

Have you ever wished that you might actually talk with some of the men and women who walked with Jesus? Have you ever wondered what they might say beyond what is recorded in the Sacred Book?

Then turn your imaginations loose and imagine that some of these have returned from the First Century and are speaking to you of the Twentieth Century.

CONTENTS

ZECHARIAH

Out of the shadows of a lifetime, bounded on the one hand by one of the greatest military men that ever lived, Alexander, The Great, and on the other hand by Jesus of Nazareth, the Prince of Peace, there emerges the figure of an old man for our consideration.

He lived between the centuries! He looked back on a day in which the maps, the culture, the language and even the dress of the world was drastically changed. He looked forward on a day in which the hearts and souls of men were drastically changed. He remembered the darkness of night that had dwelt upon his land for four long centuries, but he was privileged to see the brilliant sunrise that finally burst upon the darkened world.

But let him speak for himself. Imagine with me that this old man has returned from the ancient world and that he now stands here in my place, speaking to you:

My name is Zechariah, which, in Hebrew means "Jehovah has remembered." I spent my entire lifetime in the place of my birth—a little non-descript, unnamed village on the outskirts of Beersheba, near the Great Salt Sea. Because I was a descendent of Abijah, a priestly tribe dating back to the days of the exile in Babylon, at any early age, I, too, became a priest of the Temple. My wife, Elizabeth, was also of the priestly tribes, being a descendent of Aaron, and together we shared a happy life in our village in spite of the fact that we had no children. Because our village was situated on one of the two main highways, that led from Jerusalem to Egypt, there was always lots of excitement and activity in the village Temple. Once each year our tribe of priests would make the trip to the Holy City where we would serve in the Great Temple. Each year we would draw lots to see which

7

priest should have the privilege of burning the incense before the great altar.

Although a priest could so serve but once in his lifetime, there were many to whom the honor never came for there were hundreds of priests in our division.

But one year the lot fell to me and I prepared to offer the prayers and the incense before the altar of Jehovah God. With reverence and joy, I entered the inner Temple and lifted my voice, "May the God of mercy enter the sanctuary and be pleased to accept the sacrifices of his people," I prayed. But in my heart and in the silent recesses of my mind, I was also praying for a son who might carry on my priestly duties, and bless the home of an old man.

Suddenly it was deathly still—the murmur of the crowd praying in the outer court was strangely muffled, and I heard a clear, strong voice saying, "Do not be afraid, Zechariah, for your prayer is heard, and your wife Elizabeth will bear you a son, and you shall call his name John. And you will have joy and gladness, and many will rejoice at his birth, for he will be great before the Lord."

At first I was startled; then I was afraid; and covered my eyes and shrank back from the altar, crouching in bewilderment and confusion, paralyzed into immobility by the sound of that wonderful voice. Was I imagining things or was there really the form of an angel standing on the right side of the altar?

Could I be dreaming? How could I know for sure? Ah, I would ask for a sign. "How shall I know this?" I stammered. "I am an old man and my wife is advanced in years."

There was silence for a moment as my words echoed through the Temple"...advanced in years...advanced in years...in years." And then the voice spoke again. "Because you did not believe my words...behold you will be silent...until the day that these things come to pass."

I do not know how long I stood there before the Great Altar. The incense pots had long since ceased to give off their sweet perfume, the murmur of the people at prayer had also ceased. It was growing dark.

Quickly I moved to the outer court where the people were quietly waiting. Lifting my arms to give the final blessings, I began to speak. My lips moved—but there was no sound. I was dumb! Hundreds of bowed heads were lifted and astonished eyes looked into mine, but it was no use, I could not speak even one word. I could only give the benediction with signs and gestures, and then make my way slowly through the crowd with every eye following me, on out through the gate and across the hills to my home.

The next few months were quiet ones. God fulfilled his promise to us and we eagerly awaited the coming of our son. During this time God was also visiting a kinsman of my wife, one Mary of Nazareth, who was also to bear a son according to the will of God. She, too, had her doubts; she also heard the angel say, "Be not afraid"; she, too, asked for a sign and was told of how her cousin, Elizabeth, should bear a son in her old age. Thus it was that she came to visit our humble home in the hill country—walking all the way from Nazareth in Galilee—to sit together by the hour—youth and age—talking in whispers, smiling, weeping, brooding, anticipating, and sharing in the mysterious wonder of God's ways as young Mary sang from her heart "My soul doth magnify the Lord and my spirit hath rejoiced in God my Saviour."

Eight days after our son was born, the neighbors and friends came for the christening, as you would call it, expecting, as many people do, even in your day, that the present must be governed by the past, and according to custom the boy would be named Zechariah for his grandfather.

But I had not forgotten the word of the Lord in the Temple nor the name that was to be given to our son, and calling for a tablet I wrote thereon the word "John."

And immediately my lips were opened, the spirit of the Lord came upon me once more, and I stood to give the benediction that I was unable to pronounce in the Temple long months before. But now new words came from my lips, words that are still sung across the world today:

"Blessed be the Lord God of Israel, for He hath visited and redeemed His people; And hath raised up a horn of salvation for us in the house of His servant David; As he spake by the mouth of His holy prophets, which have been since the world began, That we should be saved from our enemies and from the hand of all that hate us; To perform the mercy promised to our fathers, and to remember His holy Covenant, The oath which He swore to our father Abraham, that He would grant unto us, that we, being delivered out of the hand of our enemies might serve Him without fear, In holiness and righteousness before Him, all the days of our life. And thou, child, shalt be called the prophet of the Highest, for thou shalt go before the face of the Lord to prepare His ways, To give knowledge of salvation unto His people by the remission of their sins, through the tender mercies of our God, whereby the dayspring from on high hath visited us, To give light to them that sit in darkness and in the shadow of death, to guide our feet into the way of peace."

Little did we know that day when our son was named, that he would one day wade the river Jordan with Mary's boy, crying, "Behold, the Lamb of God."

Little did we dream that day when our joy was so complete that one day an executioner would come marching into his dungeon cell with orders from a frivolous King; little did we know that day that Mary would once again climb a Judean hill with her Jesus and two thieves.

These things were hidden from our eyes and as my "Benedictus" blessed our home and friends, I knew only the joy and happiness with which God had blessed the last days of an old man.

Yes, even as my name, Zechariah, suggests, "Jehovah had remembered" me!

And he remembers you, wherever you are in life's calendar. God is still using old men to His glory.

Oh, I know the problems of age—how easy it is to wish for the good old days, how easy to make one's mind a court of appeals where you can review yesterday's decisions and wish that they might be changed, or fondly dream of a road which you did not take.

Sometimes it seems the only thing old people can do is denounce the young—at least it assists in the circulation of their blood.

But consider, e'er I take my leave of you, how even in your history those of advanced years have served God well. In a modern analysis of four hundred great men and women in your history, one-third of them achieved their greatest accomplishments after age sixty, while a surprising twenty three percent achieved their greatest successes after age seventy. [1]

Your Clara Barton founded the American Red Cross at age sixty, while Booth Tarkington wrote sixteen novels after he was sixty years of age.

10

Daniel DeFoe wrote *Robinson Crusoe* at sixty one, Michaelangelo painted his great masterpiece on the ceiling of the Sistine Chapel at age sixty six, working flat on his back high above the floor.

Giuseppi Verdi wrote *Fulstaf* at age eighty and your great philosopher George Santayana at age eighty two said, "I have never been happier in my life."

At age eighty six John Masefield, England's poet laureate, published his latest volume of poetry and at eighty seven Alfred Lord Tennyson wrote his immortal *Crossing the Bar*, while Toscannini was giving his final performance and Konrad Adenauer was serving as Chancellor of West Germany.

At eighty eight years of age, John Wesley preached every day of the week and at age ninety Nobel prize winner Albert-Szent Gyorgyi continues to work at cancer research. Pablo Picasso is still painting at ninety one, the late Eubie Blake and Arthur Rubenstein delighted musical audiences well into their ninety's, while artist Marc Chagall and painter Georgia O'Keefe were both active at ninety-six.

Hippocrates of a more ancient day gave the medical world its oath of service when he was ninety seven years old, while Grandma Moses was still painting at one hundred and one years.

Think of your Winston Churchills, your Bernard Baruchs, your Robert Frosts and a host of others who served well in the evening of life, refusing to believe that God will spend a half century building a man or woman only to cast them on the scrap heap of life.

So, wherever you are in life's calendar, if Christ's love has warmed your home—tell somebody. If in worship you have come close to God—witness to it. If prayer has been answered in your life—say so. If Christian faith has befriended a child of yours—share it. If through Christ you have found forgiveness and the power to forgive—let someone know. If the Church has given you a chance to serve the God you love—tell someone. If God has worked a miracle in your life too, if God has worked a minute in your life—then for God's sake, say so!

In your business...as you travel...to your friends...in your home...while you play...through your church...with your lips...by your life...whenever...wherever God gives you the opportunity—say so!

And may the "Benedictus" of your life bless and heal; and your feet be guided into the way of peace.

MARY

I am Mary. For two thousand years the followers of Jesus Christ have honored me as His Mother. But let me tell you about myself.

My childhood was a happy one with many a carefree hour spent in playing among the hills of Nazareth. How I remember the beautiful sunrises over the mountains of Gilead which illuminated Mt. Gilboa to the south, where it stood guard over the plains of Esdraelon, and then bathed the olive groves of the Jordan Valley in rich, warm colors. I would think how wonderful God was to wake His world each morning in such a beautiful way. And in the evening, as my father summoned us to prayer, I would again thank God for His goodness as the radiant colors of the sunset gave way to the shadow of night.

But some other shadows fell upon our family. My father died, leaving my mother and me alone to care for ourselves and our simple home.

Now playtime became work time as the responsibilities of age became my youthful lot.

My mother secured a position in the household of a wealthy merchant in Nazareth and left each morning at dawn for her work. In the cool of the morning I would tend our little garden, prepare the meals and do the many little tasks with which every housewife is familiar. Then I would set off for the well to draw our daily supply of water.

How I looked forward to these daily visits to the well where the women of Nazareth gathered each morning. Sometimes the conversation was typical "woman talk"—about recent betrothals, the newest babies, the latest caravans and news from Jerusalem, but usually the talk was of a more serious nature concerning the latest decrees of Caesar Augustus and the possibility of war; the unbearable taxes that kept us so poor and the possibility that they might even be increased; the hot weather and the lack of rain and the possibility of famine.

In the evening when mother returned home, I would share the news of the day with her and almost always we talked of God's promise to send a Messiah who would one day restore Israel to her rightful place among the nations.

One night when we were at evening prayer, we had just repeated together the Messianic prophecy of Isaiah, when mother was summoned to the home of a neighbor whose child was critically ill. Since it might be late when she returned, I continued at prayer alone. Again and again my thoughts returned to those words, "For unto us a child is born, unto us a Son is given, and the government shall be upon His shoulder; and His name shall be called Wonderful Counselor, the Mighty God, the Everlasting Father, the Prince of Peace."

At the conclusion of my prayers, I repeated the ancient promise, "Behold, God is my salvation; I will trust and not be afraid, for the Lord Jehovah is my strength and my song; He also is become my salvation. Therefore, with joy shall ye draw water out of the wells of salvation."

Scarcely had the echo of my words died away than a great blinding light filled my tiny room, and a voice spoke to me in tones resembling a mighty chorus, and yet with a gentleness that was as personal as a mother's lullaby: [1]

"Hail, Mary! Thou that art highly favored, the Lord is with thee; blessed art thou among women."

For a moment I was stunned and wondered if I had fallen asleep. But it was not a dream for now my eyes could distinguish at the center of that blinding light, the form of an angel whose radiant countenance matched the vibrant tone of His voice.

I tried to speak, but could not; and fear clutched at my heart; and my hands trembled like one sick of palsy.

"Fear not, Mary, for thou hast found favor with God." It was as if my father had cradled me in his arms, as he used to do when I was afraid of the dark, speaking words of comfort and soothing my childish fears.

My trembling ceased and the angel spoke again: "Behold thou shalt conceive in thy womb and bring forth a Son, and shalt call His name Jesus. He shall be great, and shall be called the Son of the Highest. And the Lord God shall give unto Him the throne of His father David. And He shall reign over the house of Jacob forever; and of His Kingdom there shall be no end."

My heart leaped at the thought of becoming a mother, for every sixteen year old girl of the village dreamed of scarcely anything else. But then the full implication of the angel's word stabbed my mind awake and I blurted out: "How can this be, seeing I know not a man?"

"Fear not, Mary, the Holy Spirit shall come upon thee, and the power of the Highest shall overshadow thee; therefore also that holy thing which shall be born of thee shall be called the Son of God. And, behold, thy cousin Elizabeth, she hath also conceived a son in her old age; and this is the sixth month with her who was called barren. For with God, nothing shall be impossible."

In the silence that ensued, my mind was racing, remembering God had often revealed His will to my forefathers through an angel; and I thought especially of the boy Samuel who was about my age when God called Him. And then I was speaking:

"Behold the handmaiden of the Lord," I said, "be it unto me according to thy word."

And suddenly the angel was gone, leaving me alone in the inky blackness of my little room.

Could it have been a dream? But no, I knew that God had spoken. I even felt different somehow and there was a warmth in my soul that could not be explained otherwise.

My faith had always been a simple one, unconfused by all the arguments of our rabbis and the many details of the law which learned men debated. It was not difficult for me to accept the fact that God had given me a message. But that I should bear a son? God's Son? And when I was not yet married? What would people say? And oh, what would Joseph think?

Joseph was such a wonderful man![2] I thought of him as he would be working, even then, in his little shop behind the Temple. Joseph was industrious and hard-working and never were there enough daylight hours. So even now he would be planing the cedars of Lebanon and carving the hardwoods from the hills by the light of a smoking lamp in his workshop.

What would Joseph say? We were very much in love and our betrothal had been announced several months previously but our marriage was planned for the ensuing year. Joseph was older and wiser, strong and rugged, with a heart of gold, but would he, could he possibly understand?

And what would I tell my mother? This problem was easily solved for when mother returned a short time later, I poured out my story to her and we talked about it far into the night. As the first faint flush of dawn came tip-toeing across the hills, we had reached a decision.

Neither of us was absolutely sure what the message from the angel really meant, but I had been given one visible sign to which I could turn. The angel had said that cousin Elizabeth was to conceive in her old age and also bear a son. If this could be verified, then I would be strengthened in my faith for days ahead. If not, then I would know that it was simply a dream.

So mother and I agreed that I should visit Elizabeth. Learning that a caravan from Nazareth was leaving that day for Jerusalem, hastily I prepared for the journey and before noon was on my way.

It was a three day journey to the house of Zecharia and Elizabeth, during which I had plenty of time to think. I was only a few miles out of Nazareth when I realized that I had not even said goodbye to Joseph, but then, mother would take care of that. My memory of the angel's visit was still sharp and clear, but could it have been an hallucination after all? How could I, a virgin, bear a child, who should one day save our people?

In the midst of my doubts and fears, as I struggled to understand, I came at last to the home of Elizabeth.[3]

As my cousin greeted me warmly, my heart leaped for joy, for it was obvious that Elizabeth was with child. It was true—even as the angel had spoken and instead of the usual greeting, Elizabeth said: "Blessed are you among women, and blessed is the fruit of your womb. And why is this granted us, that the mother of my Lord should come to me? For behold, when the voice of your greeting came to my ears, the babe in my womb leaped for joy. And blessed is she who believed that there would be a fulfillment of what was spoken to her from the Lord."

And instead of my customary reply to Elizabeth, there burst from my lips the inspired song that even in your twentieth century speaks the rhapsody of my joy in that moment.

"My soul doth magnify the Lord," I cried, "and my spirit has rejoiced in God my Saviour. For He hath regarded the low estate of His handmaiden: for behold, from henceforth all generations shall call me blessed. For He that is mighty hath done to me great things and holy is His name..."

15

For three months Elizabeth and I shared our joy in their single home, until at last it was no dream and we knew that even as God had blessed our Father Abraham with a son in his old age, so God would perform what He had promised to us.

Shortly before Elizabeth's child was due, I felt a strong compulsion to return home. Upon arriving there, my first concern was of Joseph, who had been so much in my thoughts during my stay with Elizabeth. I had forgotten that Joseph had not received a visit from the angel nor had he been granted several months to think about what God had done. Thus, the news was like a bolt of lightning to him and created a chasm between us that grew greater each passing day. At last he told me that, great as his love was for me, he could not go through with the marriage. However, he would not divorce me publicly, but, to spare my feelings, he would take the second step of the law and divorce me privately.

But again, God made known His will.

One night as Joseph lay tossing in his bed, the angel of the Lord appeared to him also.[4]

The same blinding light filled his room; the same wonderful voice spoke: "...Fear not, Joseph, to take unto thee Mary, thy wife; for that which is conceived in her is of the Holy Spirit. And she shall bring forth a Son, and thou shalt call His name Jesus: for He shall save his people from their sins."

Immediately Joseph made his decision, man of action that he was. We were married quietly the next day with only our mothers in attendance and made our plans for the arrival of my Son.

Then one day there came the dreaded decree from Caesar Augustus saying that a new tax was to be added to our burden. In order that none would escape the Emperor's greed, each man had to be enrolled in his own city. This meant that Joseph must go to Bethlehem for he was of the house and lineage of David.

Since my time was near at hand, Joseph wanted me to stay with my mother until he returned, but I insisted that I be allowed to accompany him. For many months now I had been reliving the ancient prophecies concerning the Messiah and always one thing bothered me: the prophecy spoke of Bethlehem, a three day journey to the south, as the place where the Messiah would appear. Now I knew that this journey was another part of God's wonderful plan and that my Son would be born in Bethlehem.

Joseph finally consented, somewhat reluctantly, and we started

16

off several days early, in order that we might move slowly and also have time for a brief visit with Zecharias and Elizabeth and their baby son.

It was not a tiring trip, for my mind was active and my joy unlimited. Joseph was constantly worrying about me, especially when we traveled over the rugged mountainous trails; but we would comfort one another with God's promise of old; "He that dwelleth in the secret place of the Most High shall abide under the shadow of the Almighty...because thou hast made the Lord thy habitation, there shall no evil befall thee...For He shall give His angels charge over thee, to keep thee in all thy ways. They shall bear thee up in their hands, lest thou dash thy feet against a stone."

As in times past, God performed the things He had promised and at last we came to the City of David.

There was but one Inn at Bethlehem and it was already filled to overflowing with others who had returned to be taxed. But I did not mind; after all, we had slept under the stars before and we could be comfortable there again. But the kindly Innkeeper's wife, noticing my condition, provided us with a place in the stable where the clean, fresh-cut hay reminded me of the hills of Nazareth where I played as a child.

As we settled down for the night, I shared with Joseph my knowledge that our son would be born in Bethlehem. It pleased Joseph to think that his ancestry, rather then mine, would be the title by which our son would be known, for Joseph was proud of his blood lines which made him a descendant of King David.

In the quiet of the stable, disturbed only now and then by the lowing of cattle near by, I kept remembering how great a part Bethlehem had played in God's plan. Near the Inn stood the grave of Rachel where, centuries before, Jacob had erected a monument to his loved one who had died giving birth to a son. Here at Bethlehem was laid the scene of the greatest love story in all literature, where a young foreign girl, named Ruth, came to love Boaz and to present him with a son named Jesse, who later became the father of David, for whom the city was named. These and other rich memories sustained me while I rested from the long trip and prepared for the coming event.

Then my time drew near. While Joseph ran to the Inn in search of someone to help, my Son was born![5]

Who can describe the rapture of a mother who holds to her

breast her first born? Is it not ever the miracle of God, repeated again and again in every generation? But there was a special joy in my heart that night which not even Joseph could understand completely, for I knew that this Child was the long-awaited gift of God himself, and that He would be called "Jesus" for He would one day save our people.[6] Such was my rapture that I imagined that there were angel songs filling the air and a holy light filling all the stable and the Presence of God Himself hovering very near.

Little did I dream in those first ecstatic moments that God had made His own arrangements to announce the birth of His Son. You of the twentieth century know from your knowledge of science that God must have exploded a star in His Universe in the days of our Father Abraham, which suddenly broke forth in brilliance over Bethlehem that night[7]—a star that later led Wisemen from the East to our home in the stable, where they presented rich gifts that were to sustain our little family when we had to flee from the jealousy and wrath of an angry King Herod;

A Star that still symbolizes for you the gift of God's Love and that makes tired hearts beat a little faster, that keeps all men searching for the Everlasting Light;

A Star that still leads men to leave the security and warmth of their homes to travel to the ends of the earth in the Name of the Prince of Peace;

A Star that broke forth in beauty over the shepherds on the gray hills of Judea that night long ago, and which brought them to the stable where they fell on their knees in praise.

As the shepherds told their story of how God had announced the good news to them, I knew then that I had not imagined the angel chorus after all, nor had I imagined that the Presence of God was especially near that night. The hushed tones of the shepherds and their radiant faces added further to my joy and brought to mind the words of David long ago: "My cup runneth over."

As my eyes took in every detail of the scene before me, I thought: "A manger is a small place for such a great mystery of all the intangibles of life and history" and yet "the hopes and fears of all the years are met in thee tonight."

Little did I know that we would soon be on the road again with our young son, this time bound for Egypt, while the mothers of Bethlehem would be weeping over the lifeless forms of their youngest sons.

Little did I dream of the responsibilities that would later be mine in caring for my family of seven children after Joseph died, or that Jesus would more and more grow away from me, as He came to understand the mission for which He had been sent.

Never did I dream that a stark and brutal cross[8] would one day tear my heart or that God's plan of redemption would result in so much grief and suffering. But neither did I dream that a resurrection would forever display God's power and forever make the Son of God a living reality to ALL men.

Nor did it ever cross my mind that the traditions of men should one day make me so important or that men would one day worship me instead of God's Son. I was truly "Blessed of women" but only an instrument in the hands of the living God in order that His Son might be truly human, born of woman. But it is only He who can save, only the Christ who can redeem.

Leave me then with my joy and share with me my faith that God will always perform those things which He has promised.

Go now from this place like the shepherds of old, glorifying and praising Him for the things which you have heard and seen, as it has been told unto you. "For unto you is born this day in the City of David, a Saviour which is Christ the Lord."

JOSEPH

It is well that Christmas comes to us each year, reminding us of something that happened on a night long ago, when, as today, the heart of the world was filled with foreboding and fear.

Too often, perhaps, when we think of that first Christmas, we remember only the sudden light over Judean hills, the song of the angels, the promise of peace and good will, and the cry of a new-born Child.

And we forget the lands that lay beyond that circle of light that did not hear the Christmas song. Life had no meaning for the average man, the gods were dead, or at least withdrawn from human life. And for the above average men, life could only offer a philosophy of gird up your loins and be strong, for the only certain thing about life was its uncertainty. One must be "a soldier in a campaign where there is no intermission and no discharge" (Stoics). "And what is the end of it all? Smoke and ashes and a legend—or scarcely a legend." (Marcus Aurelius)

The darkness in men's minds was also reflected in industry and government. Caesar Augustus had made a bold attempt to establish his Great New Society with ruthlessness and armed might. By devious ways, in the fashion of twentieth Century dictators, he first bought himself an army. Then he got the army to elect him a consul. Next, he convinced his two arch-rivals to form a triumvirate in order to restore the commonwealth. This restoration began with the assasination of three hundred Senators in Rome and two thousand knights. Their property was confiscated and distributed to the soldiers in what we would call today "the redistribution of land."

Within a few years, Augustus had purged the government, gotten rid of his two competitors, and had become, in his own words, "the Master of all things."

Having reached the top, Augustus determined to stay there. The Philosopher Seneca tells how he stayed in power:

"Wooden racks and other instruments of torture, the dungeons and other jails, the fires built around imprisoned bodies in a pit, the hook dragging up corpses, the many kinds of chains, the varied punishments of tearing of limbs, the branding of foreheads, all represented power."

Of course, the Caesar had to keep his restless slaves under control, and almost half the Roman Empire was in slavery, but he also had to keep the other half of his restless people amused. And so there were gladiatorial games where exhibitors (today they would be called fight managers) vied with each other in the number of contestants they could expose to slaughter. Historians tell us that one put up three hundred and twenty pairs of men to fight at one time. Agrippa caused seven hundred pairs to fight in one day. But Augustus topped them all and had ten thousand men in the arena fighting each other to the death. And when the murder of men grew monotonous, the combat of men with wild beasts was introduced.

But now Augustus was growing old and cracks were beginning to appear in the imperial fabric that had been constructed at such a terrible price of toil and blood. Anarchy was waiting in the wings, although there was armed peace for the moment. There was little hope in the land; man was a puppet, a plaything of the wild and unruly forces of the world, in which there was no will or purpose, and there was much darkness.

It was also dark in Israel. For a thousand years, from Moses to Malachi, God had been present in the life of His Chosen People; a thousand years filled with history and poetry, and battle and prophecy; a thousand years in which there was always a voice speaking for or from God:

Sometimes it was a shepherd who spoke, sometimes it was a king's voice. Other times it was a farmer's voice or a city voice—

Sometimes a voice with tears in it, at other times a voice that rang like clanging cymbals of joy; sometimes it was God's voice, that "still small voice" like the rustling of the leaves on a summer night, at other times like an alarm of wild and unrestrained tempests...

But always there was a Voice. And then silence. Four hundred years of dead silence. Not a word from God. Not a single line of prophecy. Not even a glimmer of light for the darkness.

And then, amid the darkness, suddenly there burst upon the world God's Light, and the darkness has never been able to master it since.

Remembering the setting in which the first Christmas took place, let us move for a moment inside that circle of light and through the eyes of one who was a participant in those eventful days, recall the meaning that Christmas still has for us.

Imagine with me now, if you will, that from Bethlehem there has returned across the centuries a man who now stands here, in my place, speaking to you.

I am Joseph, a descendant of King David yet a man who made his living with hammer and nail as a carpenter. When I was a young man, hard times fell upon our little village of Bethlehem and I was forced to travel north into Galilee in order to make a living. It was some years before I was able to support a wife and home, but one day I fell in love with a beautiful young girl. She, too, came from a deeply religious home and was able to see something more in me than my gray hair and calloused hands.

Mary and I were soon engaged to be married. Then, like a bolt of lightning on a cloudless day, I discovered she was going to have a child. You can only imagine what I thought—how I felt! I would not hurt her for anything—the divorce would be handled privately—but the hopes and dreams of all the years came tumbling down around me.

Only a distinct message from God assured me that it was His will for me to take Mary as my wife, and as a God-fearing man I thus accepted my place in the divine drama and remained obedient to the will of God, although, for the life of me, I could not understand it, then.

Soon after we were married, Caesar Augustus, the ambitious emperor who found Rome brick and left it marble, decided that some men were getting by without paying their taxes. Therefore, he would take a census and every man must report to the place of his birth to be enrolled.

Mary and I were not happy about this, for it was a long, arduous journey from Nazareth to Bethlehem, and she was soon expecting her baby. But it had to be done. Actually, we would both be happy to escape the gossiping tongues and slanderous neighbors who had made life so miserable for us in Nazareth.

And so we arrived late one night in Bethlehem. A group of camel drivers were gathered about a great fire in the innyard, relieving the monotony of their labors in ribald revelry and song. In the lobby of the Inn a band of Caesar's soldiers who were present to do the enrolling, gambled and drank the hours away. Beyond, the sprawling village was brightly lighted from end to end and the streets were filled with hundreds of people looking for rooms. But there were no more rooms—every place was taken.

But the kindly innkeeper's wife offered us the use of their stable for the night and we accepted readily. Mary did not seem to mind—after all, the people of Galilee often slept out under the stars, and at least we would have a roof over our heads until we could find better lodging.

And thus it was that Jesus was born in that stable that night, and his first cradle was a manger. Of course, it bothered me that, as His father, and a carpenter at that, I had no time to make a cradle for the baby.

How prophetic it would be of One who throughout His mission in life would not have a place to lay His head!

You know very well the events that took place in Bethlehem

that night. You will be observing them these days in pageant and song like the angels, in worship and adoration like the shepherds, and in the giving of your gifts like the wisemen.

But as with men in my day, you, too, may be swayed, more than you know, by material things and a philosophy of emptiness. You, too, may have doubts about the silence of God and be tempted to agree with some of your own too wise young theologians that "God is dead." Despair may also touch your hearts this Christmas as nation strives with nation in wars they can neither win nor lose, and many hopes and dreams of all your years come tumbling down around you.

It is good for you, therefore, to pause in life's press and throng to remember that "the hopes and fears of all the years" met in Bethlehem that night long ago.

In a day when space ships are being blasted into orbit and other space ships, with loved ones on board, come crashing to the earth; in a day when your young men are being killed one by one in defense of freedom, and yet the problems of people and governments and industry are discussed in terms of billions, I know you are not particularly interested in one man who lived a long time ago as a carpenter in Nazareth. But I know you are interested in One who for a time lived as a carpenter in my shop.

God in His wisdom gave me only a few short years with the boy Jesus, just long enough for me, in my simple way, to be to Him and to our other children, the best father I knew how to be.

And I like to think, that as no other religion in man's history has the image of Almighty God as a "Father," when Jesus taught men to say "Our Father" my little role in God's plan for the ages was important. And do not the fathers of the world still play a vital role in interpreting to their children the Fatherhood of God?

As you come to probe the deep mysteries of God's greatest gift of love, and as you gather in your homes and churches this Christmas time to share the ageless story of His birth, remember those even of your own number, who still live outside the circle of light, those for whom there is no justice and no hope—just darkness still.

Remember those for whom the only Voice of God they will ever hear is your voice, speaking to God or speaking for God.

"Amid the darkness (that night long ago) the Light shone, but the darkness did not master it." Not then, nor now.

And the task remains for all who cherish the Christmas story, not as a lovely legend but as a revelation of God's purpose for all people, to see that the darkness does not master the Light for you!

THE INNKEEPER

My name is Ezra Bar Jonah. I was born in a small village south of Jerusalem, lived all my life in a small village south of Jerusalem, and died in a small village south of Jerusalem.

You may not recognize my name because it does not appear in your Bible. The only thing that is mentioned there is a small piece of real estate which I owned. You see, I was the Innkeeper in Bethlehem of Judea.

One night my Inn was full of people: his Honor, Marcus Aurelius and his scribes who were taking the census; honorable men from farthest Galilee, come to Bethlehem to be enrolled; high ladies and their lords; the rich, the rabbis; such a noble throng as Bethlehem had never seen or would probably ever see again. There they were, close-herded with all their servants, until my Inn was like a hive at swarming time, and I was fairly beside myself.

How could I know, then, that they were so important, just the two, no servants or baggage, just a workman sort of man with calloused hands leading a donkey on which a pale young woman was seated.

Actually, I did not see them, for my desk clerk had already turned them away. But my wife Leah was in the lobby and, gentle women that she was, she observed that the young girl was ready to have a child and could not be turned away into the cold of night.

Quickly she escorted them to a haven in my cattle barns and made them comfortable for the night.

But even if I had seen them, how could I have known? Were Inns to welcome stragglers from Beersheba to Dan who could not pay for lodging? We would soon have been bankrupt.

And how could anyone have known? There was a sign, they said, a resplendant new star in the heavens, but I had no time for stars. And some claimed to have heard angels singing out on the hills, but how was I to hear amid the thousand clamors of my Inn?

Of course, if I had known who they were, and who it was that should be born in my stable that night, I would have turned the whole Inn upside down, his Honor Marcus Aurelius and the rest, and sent them to the stables.

Later I learned that he was born a king, a second David who would ransom us from the invaders from Rome; who would feed an army with a single loaf of bread and, if a soldier fell, but touch him and he would leap to life again. But I did not know, then.

The irony of it all was that I had been searching for the Messiah all my life. As a business man I made a fairly good living by the standards of my day, complaining all the while, as you do, about government controls and taxes and inflation. But at least we were at peace. Caesar's "Pax Romana," his "Great Society," had brought something of peace and prosperity to our land. Yet I thirsted for God. I wanted my life to have meaning. There must be something more than just food for the belly, cash for the wallet, and a tomb for the body. I hungered for freedom. I craved salvation for my soul. I needed a Messiah.

I tried religion. I studied and obeyed the thousand and one laws that dealt with religion. I observed the Sabbath, being careful not to walk through any field where the grass was taller than knee high, for this was interpreted by our religious leaders as being "work." Now don't laugh at this nonsense until you have taken a close look at some of the regulations that embody your religion.

It was not all nonsense, of course, nor is yours, and it was a great comfort to many of our people to have everything legally in order. But my soul was still hungry.

I tried business. I worked like a slave, sometimes sixteen hours a day, seven days a week; yes, even on the Sabbath where my work was far taller than my knees. But still I was not satisfied. I knew that certain luxuries of life, such as a thankful heart for

25

each new day, a sensitive spirit toward all mankind, and a courageous outlook on the valley of death, are not to be bought in the market place. And I was still searching.

I tried politics. If God was not to be found in religious rituals or in the amassing of gold, perhaps He could be found in political revolution. Laws might be able to change the hearts of men.

So I joined the Zealot party, the First Century "minutemen," with plans to overthrow the Roman rule and return the Holy City to its rightful occupants. But there was little hope among the Zealots. More often there was just hatred and prejudice and bitterness and revenge. We were little more than terrorists.

Somehow I knew that the God of my fathers, the God whose praises I had sung in the Psalms of David, the God of love and compassion and forgiveness, would not be discovered in the political arena of hatred, bitterness and revenge.

So I was still searching for answers when a Star stood over the manger in my barn where a Child was born. A few days later, the census takers scattered across the Province and some semblance of peace returned to my Inn. It seemed like a good opportunity to make a short visit to Jerusalem to lay in a supply of wines and meat. I instructed my servants to take care of the young couple in the barn, while Leah and I were gone, and to provide them quarters in the tiny room under the stairs. At least I could do that much for them.

In the Holy City there was great excitement and much talk about three Wisemen from the East who had come to Herod searching for a new born King of the Jews. They had been told that the Child was to be born in Bethlehem according to the prophets, and so the Eastern kings had ridden out to my little village. Cutting my business short, we rushed back to the Inn to see if it was true.

Yes, the Wisemen had been there just two days ago. Everyone said it was something to behold. But now they were gone. The Star was gone. The couple and Child were gone. Two gold pieces on my desk were the only bits of evidence that they had ever been there in the first place.

"The census had lined my purse with gold, But what is wealth to one grown old?

The Messiah had come just as prophets had said, And my cattle stall had been His first bed."

If only I had known!

I'd have named my Inn for love of Him "The little King of Bethlehem."

As I leave you now, to continue my journey, let me leave with you a question or two. My story is an eternal parable of the human soul: Why is there so little room for the Christ?

Have you seen him stranger? And perhaps again may see Him? Prithee, say for me "I did not know." And if He comes again, as He will surely come, with retinue and banners and an army, tell Him, my Lord, that all my Inn is His to make amends. Alas! Alas! To miss a chance like that. My Inn might now be chief among them all—if I had only known.

Have you no room for Him? Do you grieve at all that it is so, and then go busy on your way with no more courtesy than they who turned the Lord away? Are your lives so full with religion, business and politics that you grant Him space so small, less than a manger stall?

Be careful how you look upon the manger Child. He will only take the place you offer Him. How does the Son of God fare with you? Is there room in your heart for Him? Do you welcome His intrusion into your life, so filled with a multitude of things?

And do you really love Him—? Or do you just go on hating the Romans, or the Arabs, or the Jews, while worrying about the price of oil or what the stock market is doing?

Tomorrow starts today. People move. Cities grow. Times change. In the name of God you must do better than before. The future will not wait.

I know! For I am Ezra Bar Jonah, once an Innkeeper in Bethlehem, that small village south of Jerusalem.

But you are the Innkeeper now.

HEROD

I am Herod. For nearly two score years I was king of the Jews, although I myself was not a Jew. There are seven Herods in your Scriptures so you may confuse me with my son or with one of the other Herods. Let me tell you a little about myself.

I was born of royalty in the land of Palestine, where my father had been appointed ruler by Julius Caesar and where he reigned until his death at the hand of an assassin.

As you might surmise, I was a spoiled child, forever getting my own way and being denied nothing. This was also true of my three brothers and my sister.

When I was twenty-five years of age, my father was murdered and I was made king of Galilee, while my brother became Governor of Jerusalem. Like many of your modern day rulers, I had to have my own way. When unhappiness developed in my marriage, I simply married another woman. Then I married a third, and a fourth, and several more, including two of my nieces, until I had ten wives under my roof. Being husband to ten women and father to fifteen children, ten of them sons, made our palace a veritable civil war most of the time. In addition, there was a civil war raging in Israel where we were at war with the Parthians.

You of the twentieth Century know what war can do to people. One of my own brothers was killed; another preferred to take his own life; while my third brother plotted my death as long as he lived.

My sister married our uncle, and when he was executed for adultery, she married again, was divorced and married again, and was constantly involved in political intrigue. So, you see, you Americans didn't invent this system after all.

Eventually the national war was resolved and I was able to do some things that could not have been done previously. I began to build great theaters and amphitheaters and introduced great spectacles to the people. I prided myself on a magnificent physique and expertise with the bow and the javelin and actually took part in some of the sports. Every five years there would occur the great games, forerunners of your Olympic Games today. Wrestling and other athletic events would fill the theaters, along with musical contests and even chariot races. Then, in the fashion of Rome, I introduced lions and other wild beasts and eventually human contests with animals. At one time there were two thousand and five hundred slaves killed in a great spectacle.

The Jews opposed all these things, so to placate them I built a great Temple which took nearly one hundred years to complete. It always irked me that I was never remembered for the great public buildings I erected, but for the Temple which I really did not want to build at all. But at least it advanced my cause in the eyes of the Emperor and my status was guaranteed for life.

When I read your modern journals and listen to much political talk before elections, I find that it is no different in your time than in mine. If you want to get ahead in government, it pays to know the right people.

Early in my political career I came to know Marcus Antonius de Dominis, or Mark Antony as you know him. I cultivated his friendship avidly so that when Julius Caesar was assassinated, he was ready to help me take Jerusalem and become king of all Judea.

My first public act was to execute forty-five party leaders. This was simply political expediency to establish my power.

But if things of state were under control, the civil war in my palace grew worse. My sons were jealous and spiteful and cruel. They could not get along with anyone, much less themselves. Finally, I executed three of my sons, an eighty-year-old grandfather, a brother of one of my wives, and finally my wife, the Queen. Small wonder that Caesar Augustus said "I'd rather be Herod's pig than his son."

Perhaps it seems strange to you of the twentieth Century that I should become known in history as "Herod the Great." This title came to me, not because of my cunning in battle, great as that was; not for my Great Temple which has recently been discovered by archaeologists of your day; nor for my vicious temper which usually enabled me to get anything I wanted.

But around your world my name is spoken many times because

of an event that took place shortly before my death. I was seventy years of age and a disillusioned old man. Because of my murderous rage I was almost childless and deathly afraid that I, too, would be murdered. Men who rule by terror also live with terror, surrounded by evil men they cannot trust. My people did not love me, nor trust me. And I did not love them or trust anyone.

One morning I had just signed an order decreeing that at the moment of my death a score or more of leading citizens in Jerusalem should be executed. Jerusalem might not mourn for me, but Jerusalem would surely mourn when I died. Suddenly a messenger appeared with news that a King had been born in the land. This was a turn of events I had not anticipated, and you can imagine my fury and frustration when I learned later from the Wisemen of the East that "Jesus was born in Bethlehem of Judea."

Well, you know the rest of my story. The Wisemen proved to be more cunning than I, and the God of Israel protected the young King from my wrath. Though I ruthlessly murdered the new born sons of all Bethlehem as my final official act, I could not defeat the purpose of the Almighty.

As I sat alone late at night with my head in my hands, I would mumble, "Oh dear, why couldn't the wretched infant be born somewhere else? Why can't people be sensible? I don't want to be horrid...I've worked like a slave. Ask anyone you like. I read all official dispatches without skipping...I've hardly ever taken bribes. I've tried to be good. I brush my teeth every night...I'm a liberal. I want everyone to be happy. I wish I had never been born."[1]

Soon I lay dying. And there came to me a scene in the Temple when I was a young man. The Rabbi was reading from the Book of Psalms, and I could still hear his words: "The kings of the earth set themselves, and the rulers take counsel together against the Lord, and against His Annointed. He that sitteth in the heavens shall laugh. The Lord shall have them in derision."

And so I died. There was no mourning in the streets of Jerusalem for my infamous decree was never carried out. Instead, all Jerusalem rejoiced that Herod the Great was no more. What a way to die!

As my body was being carried in state to its final resting place, a Young Child was being carried in His mother's arms out of Egypt into Nazareth.

Before I leave you now, perhaps you are wondering why my story needs to be told at all. It is not a very pleasant one, I grant you.

But sometimes God uses tyrants to perform His will. Sometimes it takes a reign of terror to make men want God's "Reign of love." Sometimes the injustices of a temporary, wordly kingdom, will make people seek that Kingdom which is not of this world, and of which the angel over Bethlehem said, "of this Kingdom there shall be no end." Sometimes you people need to be reminded that the Kingdom of God will long outlast even the United States of America.

Or perhaps my life's story may say something to your guilt as you, too, stand under the judgment of God. You may never have murdered your children, but there may be a civil war going on in your home. You may never have held a gun in your hand, but for years you have listlessly condoned the bombing and killing and enslavement of defenseless people in far away lands. In this very year of your Lord, you are participating again in stirring up wars in what was once a part of my Empire; providing guns and rockets and planes to both sides.

You, too, may blame "conditions" for the unhappy state of affairs in your world. You, too, may not like what your rulers do, but perhaps it is no better than you deserve. And perhaps the violence and terror that stalks your streets and invades your homes is a kind of judgment on you.

Have you a sense of guilt? Then learn from my story that goodness will survive even when evil seems stronger. For God is the author of history. He has a stake in your world, a stake in the form of a cross and "stands within the shadows, keeping watch above His own, though right be on the scaffold and wrong be on the throne."

Perhaps God will forgive me some day for not recognizing Him when he came to my kingdom. But you are citizens of His kingdom. You gather here beneath the sign of His cross in the assurance that the Christ of Bethlehem is the answer to your yearnings, the way of pardon for your guilt, the way of peace for your fears, and the promise of life even in death.

I am Herod the Great, but not so great. Remember me only because of Him, "who was born in the days of Herod the king."

Hold on to Him, and He will hold on to you.

31

SIMEON

I am Simeon. My name in Hebrew means, "One who hears and obeys." I am a Jew. I was a Rabbi, a descendant of Jacob by his second son.

My name appears but once in your Holy Scripture and your modern biographers have summed up my life by writing of me:
> "A righteous and devout man, to whom it had been revealed by the Holy Spirit, that he should not see death until he had seen the Lord's Christ."

For three score years and ten, I had been a student of the Scriptures. Early in my life I had been convinced that God would one day reveal Himself in a Messiah, who should redeem Israel and give her back her rightful place among the nations of men.

Not long after I became a priest in the Temple, God came to me one night in the stillness of my little room, and instilled within my heart the faith that before I died, I would see the gift of His Messiah.

Now I was old and it seemed that God must have withdrawn His offer. Through the long years I had kept the lamp of prophecy burning bright, while religion was at low ebb throughout all Israel.

Could I have been mistaken? Was it just a dream?

One night I sat down in meditation to read again the ancient prophecies, and my eye fell upon the words of Malachi: "Behold, I will send my messenger, and He shall prepare the way before Me, and the Lord, whom you seek, shall suddenly come to His Temple. For I am the Lord, I change not. Therefore, ye sons of Jacob are not consumed."

Again, it seemed that God was speaking once more to my feeble heart, for truly I was a son of Jacob, and there was yet time.

And I thought how everything was certainly in readiness: We had three languages ready to carry the good news: Hebrew, Greek and Latin. Our great ancestor Moses was now being studied seriously by the Gentiles.

Socrates, the contemporary of Malachi, had broken the spell of polytheism and had prepared men to accept the doctrine of the true and living God, teaching through Plato the immortality of the soul.

Alexander the Great had brought Greek culture with him as he opened the doors of western Asia through his conquests.

Julius Caesar was building roads in Europe and in northern Africa, over which the good news could travel.

Judas Maccabeus had broken the yoke of foreign oppression and given Israel a new patriotism.

Herod the Great had built a magnificent Temple, forty six years in the building, and now the fullness of time had arrived.

Would not the Lord of the Temple soon come to the Temple of the Lord?

With my mind filled with questions and my soul troubled and anxious, at last I fell asleep. Tomorrow was another day.

Early the next morning a servant lad came to my quarters to tell me that a young couple desired the blessing for their child. This was a routine thing for a Rabbi, yet a ceremony that never ceased to cause wonder and joy in the gift of life.

As I entered the Temple, I saw a young couple standing near the altar. So absorbed were they in their infant child, that they scarcely noticed my arrival.

As I cleared my throat and smiled at them, for they both seemed quite shy, they moved quietly to the great altar and stood before me in deep reverence.

First I read to them the commandments of Moses concerning the training of a child and all that they should diligently teach their son.

Then I took the boy in my arms. There was nothing unusual about this—I had done it hundreds of times before.

And yet a strange emotion seemed to come over me, almost as if this were my son. Any father knows this feeling, who has held a new born son in his arms.

Any of your ministers knows something of this feeling, who has looked into an infant face while blessing the covenant relationship being established between parents and their God.

But this was something different, and I could not understand it. An almost overpowering sensation seemed to sweep over my soul.

There were tears in my eyes, and my throat was dry, and it took several beginnings before I could speak the familiar words of the ritual.

And then the words came, but they were not familiar. I hardly knew what I was saying:

"Lord, now lettest thou thy servant depart in peace, according to Thy word; For mine eyes have seen Thy salvation which Thou hast prepared before the face of all people; a light to lighten the Gentiles, and the glory of Thy people Israel."

As I handed the child back to its Mother, a strange radiance enshrined her face. There was not a sound to be heard anywhere in the Great Temple—and this was most unusual. Yet it seemed that angelic choruses were ready to burst forth any moment. Was my imagination playing tricks on me?

I turned back to the great Altar behind me, but there was nothing there, save the remains of the burnt offering which the couple had made.

As I stood there with indecision, suddenly, as the light of the eastern sky breaks through the shadows of night, it dawned upon my unbelieving heart that this was what I had been waiting for all these years. I had just held the Lord's Christ in my arms.

And then the meaning of my own words broke in upon my understanding. The Messiah, for whom I had waited in long, lonely vigil, was not to come as a male conqueror, but even as Isaiah had said: "Unto us a Child is born."

Here was God's light to the Gentiles: the truth about God, and man, and the life that now is and is to be; the truth that alone can banish the darkness of the world.

And here was Israel's true glory, the glory toward which all its history had been moving. Now "the glory of the Lord had been revealed" and all flesh would see it together.

And now I could die in peace, for mine eyes had seen God's salvation.

Not many days later, there was a new Rabbi in the Temple and I, Simeon, walked with my fathers, while a young couple walked the caravan trails into Egypt, cradling in their arms a Child, who would one day exchange His cradle, for a cross and a crown.

Since the fourth Century, my "Nunc Dimittis" has been the evensong of the Church, making immortal those inspired words that tumbled from lips that day long ago.

Since then, ministers of Christ have offered babyhood to God at their altars, with my joy blowing tempests in their souls.

Since that day, Christians everywhere have welcomed, with symbols of light, the birth of God's Son, believing that He still make His Advent among men.

In these days even people who give Christ no special heed, have been caught up in the deep joy of His Advent.

How about you? Have you seen the salvation of the Lord?

He comes to you to forgive, to comfort, to command, to strengthen your soul.
"For though Christ a thousand times
    In Bethlehem be born,
If He's not born in thee
    Thy soul is still forlorn.

His cross on Golgotha
    Will never save thy soul,
The cross in thine own heart
    Alone can make thee whole."

I know! For I am Simeon, "one who hears and obeys," who knows that the gift of God Himself must find room in the heart, before He finds His throne.

JOHN THE BAPTIST

I am John the Baptist. I was born in five B.C. in Hebron, a little village thirteen miles southwest of Bethlehem, and one of the oldest cities of the world that is still inhabited today.

Let me tell you about myself. In your day I would probably be known as a "P.K." meaning a preacher's kid, for my father was Zechariah, a priest in the Temple, and my mother was also a descendant of the priestly tribe of Aaron. They were both very old when God answered their prayer for a child and I was born.

At my birth, the relatives all descended on my home, even as they often do in your day, and they were insistent that I should be named "Zechariah" after my father. Names meant much more in my day than they do in yours, for a boy's name was not only a tie to the past but an indication of the future. A name was therefore no casual label nor a thing to be decided lightly.

But my father kept insisting that I should be called "John," meaning "God has been gracious." This was a brand new name and one which had no precedent in all of Israel.

You may recall that from the time an angel had told my father that he would have a son, he had been unable to speak a single word. But when the name "John" was finally made my official name, his tongue was loosed and he shouted his praise to all that were in our house. Perhaps you remember his words:

"Blessed be the Lord God of Israel, for He has visited and redeemed His people; and thou, child, shall be called the prophet of the Most High, for you shall go before the Lord to prepare His ways..."

From that time on I was known as John, son of Zechariah, and because my father continued to remind me of God's goodness, it did not disturb me unduly when the other boys in our village

36

poked fun at me on account of my strange name.

So the years passed quickly as I received my education in the synagogue school of Hebron, and came to appreciate the long history of my people and my village.

How I thrilled to the stories of Abraham, whose wife, Sara, was buried in a cave at the outskirts of town; to the tales of King David, who once reigned for seven and one half years in Hebron, and where several of his sons were born, and to the many accounts of tribesmen who fought fiercely for possession of our ten deep wells and twenty five springs, which created a lovely oasis in the midst of the surrounding desert.

Then one day, because of my father's promise to God, I made my way into that desert to prepare for my life's work. For a decade and a half, I lived alone out under the stars, searching for answers to the needs of my people, searching for God's will and for understanding of His ways. Then, God gave me a message and I knew the time had come to speak it.

It was a sabbatical year in Israel, when the fields were allowed to stand idle and the laborers had much leisure time to congregate in the villages. Thus, I had a ready audience for my message. Indeed, it was a great time to declare what God was planning to do for my people.

It goes without saying that I was rather a strange creature in my camel's hair coat and heavy leather girdle, unshaved and bearded, a little uncivilized looking to say the least. But the great crowds heard me gladly.

There are three things that make a prophet: a great man, a great message, a great time.

Obviously, I was not a famous or great man, but simply the forerunner of One who would be the greatest the world would ever know.

My message, however, was a great message, and it was a great time, for the voice of prophecy had been stilled for many centuries.

So, in the fifteenth year of Tiberius Caesar, God called me forth from the wilderness to declare "Prepare ye the way of the Lord. Confess your sins and be baptized."

At first, the people only listened politely. It was not until I began to speak sternly about the judgment that woudl be visited on the Pharisees and Saduccees, that the people began to take me seriously. No one had ever dared to lift a voice against the hypocrites who ruled the Temple, or to suggest that they, too, needed to repent of their sin.

But this was God's message, remember, and who can stand uncondemned in the presence of the Most High God?

So I reminded the people that just being sons of Abraham was not enough; for if God so desired He could raise up sons of Abraham from the very stones of the city streets under their feet.

And then when I tangled with the tax collectors, who were unpopular in my day as in yours, the people actually broke into cheers. And when they discovered that I had no fear of the Romans, who often wreaked violence on innocent people, the crowds began to ask, "What shall we do?"

"Repent of your sins and be baptized," I cried.

One day, when the largest crowd ever had gathered about me, I openly rebuked Herod the king for his evil deeds and his evil ways, for living in open adultery with Herodias, the wife of his half brother.

This time the crowd did not cheer; many eyes were downcast; there was a great silence.

But as I moved off toward the river Jordan, nearly all the people follwed me, "in great expectancy" and came down to the river to be baptized.

It rather amazed me, to tell the truth. Baptism was completely foreign to the Jew. And I never expected such a reaction to my preaching. But strange are the ways of God, His ways are not always our ways.

Concluding the baptism service, I was ready to leave when there came toward me a young man of about my own age, dressed in simple garb, with a long beard and flowing hair like my own. he stood for a moment on the river bank, looking down at me.

Suddenly, without knowing why, I cried: "Behold the lamb of God." It was a strange thing to say, and the people looked at me with wonder on their faces, but as soon as the words were out, I remembered what God had said to me in the wilderness:

"Upon whom Thou shalt see the Spirit descending, and remaining on Him, the same is He which baptizeth with the Holy Spirit."

And I thought to myself, "Could this be the Messiah who was to come?" But no! He was so young. And He didn't look the way a Messiah should look.

Before I knew it, I was knee deep in the Jordan again and He was standing along side, waiting for me to baptize Him. I thought: "If this is the Holy One of God, what need has He of baptism and repentance?"

As if He read my mind, He said quietly: "Suffer it to be so, now."

So I baptized Him, and as we moved up out of the water, it seemed as if the heavens were opening. A dove descended to rest on his shoulder and a great Voice said, "This is my beloved Son in whom I am well pleased."

I will never know if anyone else in the great crowd heard those words, but there was a joy in my heart that day which is impossible to describe.

God had kept His promise. He had sent His Son. My work was finished.

You know how my life ended. Herod openly confessed that I was a "just and holy man,, but he had to satisfy Herodias, so he threw me in prison. My death soon came in an unusual way, just as my birth had been unusual. Herodias tricked the drunken king to pronounce a death sentence, and so ends the story of my life.

And yet it is not ended, for in many ways my story is your story too.

Every man has his wilderness, whether he eats locusts and wild honey or filet of mignon and pheasant under glass; whether he dresses as a hippie or wears a knitted suit and tie.

And every man must decide for himself to what issues of life he will give himself, and where his vocation lies in relation to the will of God.

This decision does not always come in youth—sometimes it comes in maturity and in the successful conclusion of life's ventures.

But every man has his wilderness, his time of decision making, for every man has his guilt and pride with which to contend.

It was not only the Pharisee of my day who rested on the spiritual momentum of his fathers, but I note there are those in your day as well who seem to think that their acceptance in the eyes of God is based on ancestral title deeds. As the Master of Men was fond of saying, "Don't tell me about your roots; what of your fruits?"

Every man has his wilderness, every man has his guilt and pride, and every man shares the impatience that was mine.

Once I expected God to work a miracle and through the Messiah to bring in His kingdom in one bold, miraculous stroke.

But I learned that God works slowly to perform his miracles, and he most often works them through those who are willing to live, and to work, to suffer, if need be, and even to die for his purposes.

Are you ever impatient with God?

Have you ever asked, as I did from Herod's prison, "Are you the Christ, or do we look for another?"

On this side of the cross and the tomb, more than anywhere else in the world, you have your answer.

Whatever your wilderness, your pride, your impatience with God, bring to Him your heart and soul, to be touched anew by the Spirit of the living God, to find new direction for your life, to be drawn closer to Christ in the renewal of your vows to Him.
"that ears which have heard His voice,
   may be closed to the voice of clamor and
   dispute,
that eyes which have seen His great love,
   may also behold His blessed hope,
that tongues which have sung His praise,
   may speak His truth,
and feet that have walked in His courts,
   may walk in the regions of light.
And that the souls of all who shall receive
   this blessed Sacrament may be restored to
   newness of life."[1]

ANDREW

I am Andrew, the first Disciple of Jesus Christ. My name in Greek means "manly" or "brave," although I never had the opportunity to live up to my name. But let me tell you a little about myself.

My home in Bethsaida on the northern tip of the Sea of Galilee, was a famous fishing port. As you might surmise, most of the villagers were fishermen. Together with my father and my famous brother was shared a reputation for being the finest fishermen on the Sea. Not only were we successful commercially, but whenever famous Roman officials came to visit our beautiful little city, it was our boat they chartered for deep sea fishing.

Perhaps this was due, not only to our good reputation, but to the fact that my brother Simon Peter was a very colorful character, known far and wide as a flamboyant, successful Captain.

Have you ever lived under the shadow of a famous brother, or sister, or father or mother? It's not easy, let me assure you.

When I visit your homes of the twentieth Century, I often see beautiful polished brass instruments in front of your fireplaces. How they sparkle and shine. But upon closer inspection, there is often to be found somewhere in back and out of sight, an old dirty well-used poker or tongs, with which the fire is stirred when company is not around. So it was in Bethsaida. Brother Peter was the polished one—and what a show he could put on when he wanted to!

I was the quiet one, usually out of sight.

Peter was famous—I was obscure.

Peter was a born leader—I was a follower.

Peter was a Voice—I was but an echo.

Then one day something happened to reverse our roles. Let me tell you about it.

As a young man I was trained, as other boys were, in the Synagogue School of Bethsaida. There I developed an intense interest in the Scriptures, especially those that pertained to the coming of the Messiah. I had had enough of those haughty Romans with their domineering ways and longed for the day when Israel would take its rightful place among the nations of the world.

Then one day we thought the Messiah had truly come. For here was one who preached as no other Rabbi had ever preached. With a voice of thunder here was one calling our people to repentance as no other had done. Here was one with great tenderness and meaning, baptizing with water and proclaiming the coming of God's Kingdom on earth. Yet, John the Baptist, always spoke of another who was yet to come, and we could not

41

understand.

Then one afternoon, when two of us were assisting John in a service at the Jordan River, he suddenly stopped right in the middle, and pointing to a young man coming toward us on the river bank, he cried, "Behold the Lamb of God that taketh away the sin of the world."

For a moment we were a bit annoyed at the interruption, but a strange hush had fallen over the great crowd of people, and I had the feeling something very important was about to happen.

But nothing did! The strange young man just stood there with the trace of a smile on his lips and a strange light in his eyes. Then he turned away from the crowd and began to leave.

Unconsciously, I followed him up the bank, without knowing who he was, and catching up to him I said, "Rabbi, where are you staying?" Turning to me he looked deep into my eyes until I wanted to turn away. But something held me. Then he broke the spell by saying, "Come and see." So, as the afternoon shadows began to drop over the hills, two of us walked with him to the house where he was staying.

It is impossible to explain the wonders of those two hours as he opened the Scriptures to us in a way we had never known before, and at last revealed himself as the true Messiah. "I am come," he said, "that you might have life, and have it more abundantly."

We had been waiting so long for the Messiah that our hearts were more than ready to receive him. Now God at last had answered the cry of his people and had come to dwell with them.

When he sent us away with his blessing, I ran across the docks as fast as my short legs would carry me to tell the good news.

You know, when a man finds a priceless treasure, he has to tell someone about it.

When a woman has been miraculously healed of a terminal disease, she cannot keep the fact to herself.

And when one has had a deep experience of the soul, there is no keeping quiet.

I had to tell someone.

Where was my brother Peter? Then I saw him, sitting on the bow of a boat, mending nets. "Peter," I shouted, "we have found the Messiah. Quick, come with me."

Now in all honesty I must confess that Peter did not throw down the net and run across the docks to me. Rather, he threw back his head and laughed that uproarious laughter of his, finally saying, "Little brother, silly little brother, come give me a hand with these nets."

But I was not to be denied. As I continued to plead with him, something of the earnestness of my voice must have conveyed my faith, for at least he followed me, if somewhat reluctantly, and I introduced him to Jesus Christ.

Never did I realize, even in my lifetime, that this was probably the most important introduction in the history of mankind.

Have you ever introduced anyone to your Lord? Have you given up anything to be a disciple?

If so, then you know something of the thrill that was mine as Peter and James and John and the others walked with the Master of men. Leaving our fathers and our boats and our living, we burned our bridges behind us, making it impossible to do anything but go on. There was no way of retreat, but we never desired one. Like many a displaced person of your times, like many a soldier answering the call to duty, we left everything behind at the call of Christ.

Have you left anything behind in order to be his disciple? What of your prejudice, your pride, your aversion to anything new or different? Have you merely incorporated these into your faith, or have you left some of them behind?

And have you ever really introduced anyone to your Lord? It was my privilege to do so on several occasions. Once a band of Greeks came seeking Jesus. Some of the disciples muttered, "You can't trust these foreigners." Phillip, who was of Greek origin, wanted to take them to Jesus. But I did.

Another time a great crowd of people had gathered on a hillside to hear the Master speak. As lunch time drew near, they were all hungry but there was no food within miles. We began to worry about how such a large crowd could be fed. Then I remembered seeing a young boy with a picnic lunch in his pocket. So I took him up to Jesus and introduced him. The multitude was fed.

It always amazed me how the Master could meet our needs, even before we knew what they were. But of course, "he could see into the depths of human souls, souls that appeared to have no depth to careless eyes."[1] Thus proving that when God measures a person, he puts the tape around the heart.

As one of your own poets has put it: "For good ye are and

43

bad, and like to coins: some true, some light, but everyone of you stamped with the image of the King."[2]

So, some find the Christ by looking for him, but many more find him because another who knows him has made an introduction. Have you ever been the catalyst that brings together two elements that otherwise would never unite?

As I travel through your twentieth Century cities, I marvel at the things you have accomplished in this land of the free. For example, I hold in my hand an object, which those in the rear may not be able to see clearly, but those here in front can see without problems. Someone tell me what you see.

Right. A little black dot just a sixteenth of an inch square. And you see nothing else.

This little black dot represents bits. Your grandparents knew what a bit was: you put it in the horse's mouth so the animal would go where you wanted him to go. Your parents also knew what a bit was: two bits was the standard hourly wage "way back then" and would buy a couple of sodas. But the modern generation knows that a bit is related to the computer age. You can't play Pac-man without it!

Back in 1964 this old vacuum tube which I hold in my left hand, equivalent to two bits, was being replaced by sixteen bit modules such as the one I hold in my right hand. One sixteenth of an inch square, the size of the dot on the piece of paper, small enough for an ant to carry away, these bits on this module contain sixteen microscopic electronic elements.

By the time you were celebrating your National Bicentennial in 1976, some two thousand of these bits could be contained in a quarter inch square, providing stored information that could be recalled in three micro seconds. You know, of course, that a micro second is one millionth of a second, and that's pretty fast.

But today, the modern computer has two hundred and fifty six thousand memory bits, calculating in nano seconds—one billionth of a second. That's really fast.

And recently, the Japanese began talking about their megabits—one billion bits of computer memory. They went on to talk about M flops—a million floating operations per second. Sort of boggles the mind, doesn't it?

Of course many of you in this community have already learned to talk to computers and even your children are learning computer language in grammar school...three basic languages, Fortran, Pascal and Basic...and words such as bits, chips, gates, logic, menu, mask, wafer, etc. Welcome then to the Hi-Tech era with a brand new language and exciting days ahead.

Of course there will still be problems, some of them small problems, such as trying to explain to your eight-year-old what "counter-clockwise" means when he's wearing a digital watch!

Now most all of you within sight of the little object I held up a few moments ago, saw that little black dot. But no one indicated that they also saw a large otherwise empty piece of paper. And that's my speech this morning.

The Creator in His wisdom has given you a brain to develop and train and use. Like the piece of white paper, it is far greater than any bit or chip.

In the great public Library of New York City, there are ten million books on the shelves. If you were a fast reader and could read one book a day, it would take you seventy years to read those ten million books.

But it would take twenty million books to record in English the thoughts and memories of just one human brain.

And someone has determined that to build a computer which would duplicate that human brain, would require an area as large as Grand Central Station to house it; the electrical power of a city the size of Washington, D. C. to run it; and the amount of water that flows over Niagara Falls in just one day to cool it.

Now the human brain weighs only about three and a half pounds but has approximately fifteen billion bits of memory. It requires no special housing, no special electrical power, and no water to cool it. It is beyond imitation, and somewhat cheaper to produce!

And for that page of life upon which you are writing, the Creator has not only given you a brain, but he has also given you a touch of his spirit, the ability to think his thoughts, to speak his words, to do his will in the world where you live.

You do not have to be brilliant in science or math or politics or finance or government in order to play your role. But good or bad, like coins, everyone of you is stamped with the image of your King.

How then will you write on life's page? Hi-Tech is just a tiny speck on that page of life. The march of science and knowledge and intelligence will go on, uncovering heretofore unknown realities that have existed all around us from the beginning of time. But there is no reason to downgrade the heart and soul of mankind.

Today, as engines of apocalyptic destruction are being wheeled into place in Central America, Europe, Russia, the Middle East and the Orient, there is yet throughout your world a dawning sense that the people of the world must become the proper custodians of their planet.

Spiritual resources are available, the same resources that enabled twelve ordinary men, including one Andrew, to turn the world upside down—or perhaps for the first time to turn it right side up.

As you continue to train and use your brain, and to fill the page of life that God has given you, wherever you are in life's calendar, may the spirit of the living Lord, whose image you bear, possess your life.

Freed by technology in days to come from much of life's drudgery, may you have time to allow your creative nature to grow.

"May explorations of new worlds in space be matched on earth by a new search for meaningful relationships between families and peoples and nations.

For unless you do something violent and stupid with your future, the eternals of hope and faith and love and laughter will still be there."[3]

So maybe, just maybe, you may be instrumental in turning the world right side up again. I know. For I am Andrew, who once lived under the shadow of a famous brother, but who really lived in the shadow of Jesus Christ the Lord.

PETER

The most famous of men are usually remembered for their greatness more than their weakness. Most often they are portrayed by historians at that point in life where their wills were tempered, their convictions moulded, and their past failures converted into victory.

Seldom are we permitted to witness the struggle of a man's soul, his contest with conscience, his duel with doubts, his frustrations with faith, his temptations of thought, his struggle of spirit.

Usually, biographers edit the uncertainities and dilemas, the vacillations and fallabilities of men's lives, to show only the courage and conviction which eventually crowned such a life.

Not so, however, in the Gospel. Here we are priviliged to see, long before such men were numbered with the saints, the sparring of mind, the striving of body, the strife of the soul.

And from the Gospel record, as well as today, there are many such Voices that call to us. Sometimes we wish that we might actually hear these voices of the First Century—we wonder what they would say to us.

Give free reign to your imaginations for a few moments then, and imagine with me that there has returned from that first Century a man who now stands here in my place, speaking to you:

I am Peter, Disciple and Apostle of Jesus Christ, a man with two personalities and four names, the only one of your Holy Scriptures to bear the name Peter.

But let me tell you about myself.

I war born in Bethsaida, which means "House of fishing," on the northern coast of the Sea of Galilee. As you might surmise, my father was a fisherman, even as his father before him.

My boyhood was spent along the famous fishing docks of the city and along the banks of the river Jordan, which rose in the mountains to the north where Mt. Hermon, majestic and regal, towers like a fortress over the plains, and from whence the Jordan flows into the Sea of Galilee near Bethsaida.

Some years later we moved a few miles down the coast to Capernaum, where I established a home for my wife and her mother, and for my bachelor brother Andrew.

Like my father, my family was religious. However, to me the worship of the Synagogue seemed a waste of time—time that could much better be spent in repairing ships and fishing nets from which we made our living.

How proud I was of my fishing fleet! It was the finest anywhere on the sea. And naturally I was proud of the fact that I had earned my reputation of being the best Captain and the most successful fisherman in the whole area. And all of this in spite of the fact that I never had much education.

While I was neither a devout man, nor an educated man, I was passionately proud to be a Jew, and felt myself somewhat superior to the Greeks among whom we lived and worked.

As a Jew, I shared the hope of my people, that one day a Messiah should come to rescue us from the yoke of the oppressor. But since our prophets had been predicting this fact for centuries, I was not overly optimistic about any such thing happening during my lifetime.

Then one day, my brother Andrew came running across the docks, shouting at the top of his lungs, "We have found the Messiah!"

Now I was sure that my little brother was suffering from the heat, but since business was slack and it was too hot to work, I followed him, half out of idle curiosity.

In a few moments we were standing in the presence of Jesus of Nazareth. Suddenly I felt very unsure of myself. Now I feared no man—be he Emperor or peasant—but this man looked different from any I had ever seen. He spoke in a different way. He WAS different.

For a moment He looked into my face with just the touch of a smile on his lips, as if He had been expecting me all the time. Then, the smile gave way to a more intense look, and He spoke:

"So you are Simon, son of John?
You shall be called Cephas."

At first I was resentful that any man should have the audacity to change my name. Who did He think He was anyway? I was born Simon, son of John, even as my playmates had been known as Simon, son of James, or Simon, son of Joseph, and Simon I would remain.

But my resentment quickly passed, for there was authority in this Voice, an authority that caused my spine to tingle and my anger to recede.

"Follow me," He said, "and I will make you fishers of men."

And follow Him I did, together with Andrew and two others of our crew, James and John, the sons of Zebedee. With scarcely another thought for the operation of our fleet of ships, which we had labored so long to obtain, we followed Him.

Such was the power and authority of His Person.

Since you are well acquainted with the events of those days that centered around the ministry of Jesus, where I was privileged to be one of the inner circle, let me pass over them quickly just now, and bring you to a scene that is as important to you as it was to me.

Jesus had healed a blind man in my native city of Bethsaida, and we were walking along the Damscus highway on the road to Caesarea Phillipi, when stopping suddenly, Jesus asked, "Who do men say that I am?"

His question caught us unaware and unprepared. By common consent, I had become the representative and spokesman for the disciples whenever we wanted to say anything to Jesus. It was not until much later that I became the spokesman for Him to other men.

But while I was searching for some kind of an answer, others of the disciples blurted out:

"Some say you are John the Baptist, come back to life."

"Some say you are the prophet Elijah."

"Others say you are one of the prophets."

"But who do YOU say that I am?" Jesus asked.

There was an awkward silence, during which His eyes roved over the group and came at last to rest upon me.

Well, who WAS He? I had spent nearly every waking hour of the past three years with Him—certainly I ought to know who He was. But did I?

At last I replied, "You are the Christ."

In your twentieth Century, knowing who the Christ really is, you might well imagine that I fairly thundered those words of affirmation.

But let me confess to you that I did no such thing.

Actually, to the best of my memory, my words formed a question. Certainly, there was a question in my mind.

"You...are...the...Christ?"

And quickly came the reply "Blessed art thou, Simon, son of John,...you are Peter, and on this rock I will build my Church."

I, Peter, a rock? What a laugh. From Bethsaida to Gaza and from Jericho to Joppa, my reputation was that of inconsistency and contradiction.

In one moment I could match the fury and violence of the most boisterous and profane sailor, and in the next be as placid and unruffled as the plodding Philip, who, from the days we first swam and played together as boys in Bethsaida, never got excited about anything.

No, there was nothing in my make-up, even by the wildest stretch of the imagination, to indicate that I could ever be a rock.

Once I had tried to show my strength by walking to Him on the water, only to find myself drowning in the darkness of my own fears, until He stretched out a saving hand to me.

And although I did not know it at the time, within a few short hours I would so tempt the Master that He could call me "Satan."

And within a few short weeks, I would boast of dying before I would ever deny Him, only to deny Him three times in one night, when a servant girl laughed in my face.

No, there was nothing rock-like about me and everyone knew it, including Simon Peter.

Therefore, the Church of which the Lord spoke must be built on the rock of my confession rather than on the rock of a man, and on that same confession as others would make it through the years, even when it might be spoken as a question.

It was my privilege, of course, to know Jesus as few have ever known Him—to see His love and compassion for all men; to witness His strange power; to be caught up into a Spirit that truly was not of this world.

And I knew what He had done for me, that He was indeed much more than a prophet, much greater than John the Baptist. But was He truly the Messiah? The Christ of God? How could a man be sure?

50

"Thou...art...the...Christ?"

"Thou art Peter, Rock."

If I could scarcely believe my own ears, He believed me, and recognized the magnitude of my half-hearted confession.

But so it has ever been: man's faith, a faltering, stumbling, fickle thing—just a mustard seed; and Christ's love, a powerful, saving thing, taking our confused questions, our stuttering confessions, our feeble faith, and even by the most tentative belief, calling men and women into His Kingdom.

God DOES work in mysterious ways. Seldom are we "stung by the splendor of a sudden thought" or led to faith by sheer reasoning power. Seldom do we come face to face with the Christ through the example of others or with a complete knowledge of who He is.

Rather, we come as children; not quite sure, but wanting to know; not quite certain, but believing there is no other answer.

And He accepts us just as we are—with all our dullness and limitations.

"Who do you say that He is?" then. Idealist? Teacher? Sentimental character? Moralist? Social Crusader? A picture on the wall?

It matters not what you call me—Simeon, Simon, Cephas or Peter, and it does not matter too much what my confession was.

The one thing that does matter is how you give answer to that question, "Who do you say that I am?"

As you break the Bread and drink the Cup, which speak of His death and His living Presence as Lord and Savior, bring with you your questions, your doubts, your feeble faith, to be touched by the power of His Spirit.

For it could be that the Lord of life is waiting here this morning for some one to confess "Thou art the Christ."

Commit to Him whatever faith you have, however fragile and tentative your belief may seem to be, and it will be magnified and multiplied many times over by the power of God.

I know! For I am Peter, whose rough, calloused hands, by the power of God, became the healing hands of a saint; whose wild, restless spirit, by the miracle of love, at last found wings to the very throne of God.

SIMON ZELOTES

I am Simon Zelotes. You will not find anything about me in your Bibles, save that I was listed as one of the twelve disciples. So let me tell you a little about myself.

I was born in the little village of Nain, which nestles in the foothills of Mount Tabor, five miles southeast of Nazareth. My youth was spent among the olive trees and fig groves which flourished around our village, where I worked from sun-up to sun-down to support my widowed mother.

When I was but a child, my father was killed in an argument with a Roman soldier and from that day I hated the sight of a Roman, and determined to do everything in my power to avenge my father's death and drive the oppressors from the land.

When I was sixteen years of age, I was accepted into the Zealot party, and hence my surname Zelotes, meaning zealot. This was the last of the great Jewish parties to emerge in our history. Herod the Great had died several years previously, having held our nation together by the power of his personality and the skill of his diplomacy, just as Eastern leaders do in your day.

But his two sons did not have their father's ability and soon Rome appointed one Cyrenius to be governor, to collect additional taxes from the people and to divide us in our loyalty.

Thus it was, then, that there emerged a group of men with "an inviolable attachment to liberty" claiming, "God is the only ruler and Lord." (Josephus)

Many of us who wanted adventure, who felt that life was rather dull, and who hated the Romans, seized the opportunity to enlist in the Zealot Party. I suppose you would call us revolutionaries.

It is true that many a night I would slip out of my house around midnight, make my way through the back alleys of the village in order to dodge the ever-present Roman sentries, climb over walls, crouch in breathless silence behind trees, dash for the cover of an olive grove, lie flat on the ground with my heart pounding in fear of discovery, scramble across moors and hills, down steep ravines—

Then a password, a forced march, and a bloody strike on some undermanned Roman outpost.

Oh at first we were simply young men with a cause and a keen social conscience, who were dissatisfied with conditions, and wanted a change in our nation. But our cause soon attracted men of violence who were extravagant and reckless in the worst way, each carrying a concealed dagger in his belt, welcoming open warfare against Rome, against the Gentile, yes even against a brother Jew. Small wonder that we soon came to be known as "the Assasins."

But any reading of history should convince you that something had to be done. Here were the Publicans in our midst, willing to sell out to Rome in order to grow rich from the misery of their fellow men. Here were the Sadducees, willing to strike cynical bargains with a foreign power and to use that power for their own ends. Here were the Essenes, willing to withdraw from life in passive contemplation, devoting themselves to piety and avoiding all responsibility.

Do you wonder that some of us rebelled as patriots? Or do you forget the Liberty Boys and the Minute Men, who were roused to action over taxation in the early days of your nation, and who went on to resist those deeper and more complex problems of your Colonial society?

A few years ago, you might not have understood my deep feelings and my revolutionary spirit, but today in nearly every part of your world, you see young men and women brushing aside reason and prudence, while giving vent to long repressed feelings and resentments. They, too, are easy prey for the violent ones who often take over a cause, but there are times when some must speak aloud what others feel in their hearts. And so we Zealots blew upon smoldering coals to fan them into blazing flames.

Using the battle cry of Mattathias Maccabeus, one of our great National heroes, we cried:

"Let every one who is zealous for the law, and supports the covenant, come out.."

53

"No God, but Jehovah; no tax but to the Temple; no friend but a Zealot," we cried, and terror became the mood of the hour.

At one point the hills of Galilee were covered with smoke for two whole months, and the people of the villages huddled together in fear for mutual protection.

Eventually, the strong arm of Rome put down our rebellion and those of us who managed to escape with our lives went underground. Without a cause and without a leader, there was little hope left.

Then a man from nearby Nazareth appeared in the Holy City and began to excite our people once again. Here was one who apparently had the courage to stand up to corrupt rulers of the Temple, as well as to the armed might of Rome. Again our hopes began to rise.

One day I risked discovery and arrest by going to hear Him preach in the synagogue at Nazareth. Where did He get such wisdom? Where did these strange powers come from? Wasn't He just a carpenter's son in the little village?

I wanted to know more so I followed Him to Capernaum, along with four young men He had already chosen to be His helpers. But I followed at a safe distance.

Never shall I forget that Sabbath Day in beautiful Capernaum, for it was truly a day of miracles. First He preached again in the Synagogue, and never had I heard such words in my life. Then, right before our eyes, He healed a man with an unclean spirit, a little later He healed the mother-in-law of the Big Fisherman, Peter, and then a host of others who in rapid succession swarmed around Him, crying, "Thou art the Son of God."

It was confusing, I must admit. I lay awake most of the night thinking about what He had said and what He had done. Early the next morning, as the first touch of dawn began to break over the eastern hills, I steathily made my way out of the city, my mind filled with many things and my heart strangely warmed.

Suddenly, on the road before me stood the figure of a man, faintly outlined in the last vestige of darkness. Fear touched my heart, that it might be a Roman soldier, but in a moment I recognized that unmistakable figure of the prophet of Nazareth.

I started to speak, but no words came. I started to move toward him, but my feet seemed anchored to the ground. Then He said simply, "Simon Zelotes, follow me."

And I did! And I have been following Him ever since.

You remember, I said it was a day of miracles and perhaps the greatest miracle that day was that Jesus took me, "the flaming one" with a dagger at his belt, with nervous hands, with eyes of blue steel—He took ME into the circle of His friends.

A few days later I almost wished that I had not thrown away my dagger. We paused for a moment at the seat of customs where Jesus began to talk to a publican named Levi. I had once taken an oath to kill any publican I met, and unconsciously my nervous hands fumbled at my belt for a dagger that was no longer there.

And before long, the dagger in my heart also disappeared. Another miracle took place as Matthew joined our band: All personal enmity was destroyed by the love of Jesus Christ.

And what happened to me after that? I remained an Apostle on the other side of the cross, and with the Apostle Jude took the Gospel to Persia. Eventually we were martyred there for the cause which had claimed our lives, and so I died.

Before I take my leave of you, let me share with you two or three things that I learned in the transformation of my life:

First, I learned that there is no cause anywhere in the world greater than the cause of Jesus Christ.

Men of your day, trying hard to relax and enjoy their leisure, often find life one long, meaningless routine and become bored to death.

Others seek the way of violence, as once I sought it, or the way of passive unconcern, as some in my day did, but there is still no cause in the world like the cause of Christ.

Fortunately, in this cause you do not have to work out your own salvation by your own brilliance. You do not serve in this cause because you are qualified. You do not build a kingdom according to your own blue prints or plans. But you serve for just one reason:

The Son of God has laid His hand upon you in grace, and has said, "Come, follow Me. Come as you are, in your old clothes, even with a dagger at your belt, or in your heart, but come, follow."

The second thing I learned was that if Matthew the Publican and Simon the Zealot could live at peace with each other within the intimate band of twelve men, then there is no breach anywhere between men, that cannot be healed when men love Christ enough.

Sure there are many tensions in your day, as there were in

mine. Zealots blow upon smoldering coals in The Middle East, while others fan into blazing flames the ancient prejudices of men in New York City and in Smithville. How many there are who can see but one color of the rainbow and never see all seven.

So suspicion and prejudice still divide men from their brothers, as they hide from one another behind man-made curtains.

But there is no breach anywhere between men that cannot be healed when they learn to love Christ.

The third thing I learned was how much more thrilling it is to build something, than to tear something down.

Recently I wandered down your Market Street
    To see what kind of men I'd meet.
I saw some there—tearing a building down
    A busy gang in a busy town.
The spectators crowded ever nearer
    To watch with interest the end of an era;
As with crane and ball and lusty yell
    The worked their will and a building fell.
I asked the foreman, "Are these men skilled,
    And the men you'd hire, if you had to build?"
He laughed in my face and said, "No, indeed,
    Just common labor is all I need
To wreck with ease in a day or two
    What builders have taken years to do."
And I thought to myself as I went my way:
    Which of these roles do Christ's men play today?
Are they builders, who work with utmost care
    Measuring life, yet ready to dare
To shape their deeds to the Master's Plan
    And build His kingdom throughout the land?
Or, are they wreckers, who walk the town
    Content with the labor of tearing things down?

I am Simon, the Zealot, who learned to build rather than destroy; who learned to love rather than to hate; who learned that you cannot change the Christ into a zealot but that he can turn you into a disciple; who learned that his love can forever change men's hearts, and harness flaming spirits to the will of God.

MATTHEW

Have you ever wanted to write a book? Every now and then each of us dreams of being an author, I suppose, and of writing deathless poetry or prose that shall live on in the hearts and mind of men. Few of us ever do, of course, but we can dream.

Many years ago there lived a man who never even dreamed of writing a book and who was quite certain that no one would ever want to remember him for long. But his life was suddenly changed and the history of his times, which he wrote with his own hand, today heads the list of best-sellers.

I am Levi. I was born in the year three thousand seven hundred and seventy in the city of Capernaum, and was named for the third son of Jacob. All my life was spent in this beautiful, tropical village on the northern shore of the sea of Galilee.

My youth was uneventful and differed little from that of my friends, save that I was able somehow to get along with the Romans who ruled our city and nation and did not hate them quite as much as most Jewish young men did.

Thanks to my father's wealth and influence, I was able to purchase a lucrative business—that of tax collector. The title that went with the office was "publican," which, in Latin, designated one who handled public finance.

The people of my day did not like taxes any more than you of the twentieth century! They believed it was lawful to pay tribute only to God, and therefore they deeply resented the many taxes imposed upon them by Rome.

And, believe me, the Romans were past masters at creating new ways to tax the people. There were the standard taxes on the land, requiring ten percent of all grain raised in the fields, and twenty percent of all wine, fruit and oil. Every man from the age of fourteen years through age sixty five had to pay a poll tax amounting to one day's pay per year and also an income tax of one percent. Compared with your modern income taxes, perhaps this seems quite negligible to you, but consider the many other special taxes our people had to pay:

For example, the import-export tax sometimes ran as high as fifty percent. Everyone who used a highway, a bridge, a harbor or a stall in the market, had to pay a tax, which was assigned and collected by the publicans.

The publican also collected a sales tax, a tax on all licenses issued to traders, a tax on anyone who crossed a city, including a tax on the merchants cart, a tax on the beast of burden that pulled the cart.

In fact, if a stranger even so much as walked into a walled city, he was charged a tax!

Nor could a man die in peace. For the Romans had dreamed up a "death duty" which you of the twentieth Century somehow have not yet discovered, although you do have your inheritance taxes.

In the collection of all these and many other taxes, the publican always collected much more than he turned over to the Roman officials and his office might better have been entitled "extortionist."

Indeed, the Jews had many such names for us and did not hesitate to use them at every opportunity. The publican was so despised that he was forbidden to worship in the Temple. By law he was forbidden to be a witness or a judge. Compared to your twentieth century, he had the social status of a quisling, an outlaw, a bootlegger or a gambler.

And yet, it was well worth it for it did not take long in the seat of the customs to become an extremely wealthy man.

Or was it worth it? Often I would lie awake in the silence of the night hours wondering if it really was worth it. I was learning that money would not buy everything. We had no neighbors and no real friends; no social life; no religious life at all. We did have a magnificent home, with many servants, but no one ever came to call. My wife had many beautiful clothes to wear, but no place to wear them.

My son and daughter had a good education and much leisure time, but no one with whom to enjoy these things. Ours was indeed a lonely life.

But we adjusted to it somewhat. Because I was barred from the Temple and its worship, I began to spend much time in searching the Scriptures, particularly those that told of a promised Messiah. Like every good Jew, I looked forward with eagerness to the day when God would redeem Israel from the oppressor and establish us as the Chosen of the earth.

One day I was seated, as usual, at my place in the customs on the great Damascan highway that came through Capernaum. I had just completed a long and bitter argument with a wealthy Samaritan trader, who had tried to slip by without paying his taxes. I was, therefore, somewhat irritated when a noisy crowd of people approached my station.

In the center of that crowd was a distinguished looking young man of about my own age. He had the poise and bearing of a king and for a moment I considered giving an order to my Roman guards to bring him to me for taxing. But then I noticed that all His followers were illclad and obviously peasants who could pay but little into my coffers. Besides, it would not be worth another argument just now.

As I started to turn away, the young man turned and looked at me and smiled. "Not an unusual thing," you say. But it was! This was the first time in more than five years that anyone had ever smiled at Levi.

Before I could even get to my feet, He was gone and I was left with only the lingering warmth in my soul which His smile had produced.

Later I learned that He was an intinerant preacher out of Nazareth, named Jesus, and that He often preached in Capernaum, which had become His second home.

Several weeks later I heard Him preach. Again and again I went back, for no man ever preached as this Man did. And always His eyes seemed to seek me in the crowd, and always there would be the trace of a smile and the responding warmth in my soul.

Then one day I learned that He had healed the mother-in-law of Simon, the big fisherman, and later the same day I met a boyhood friend who for years had been bedridden with palsy and who now moved about freely without the trace of a tremor, because He had met this Jesus. Others told me how He had even forgiven sins and it was this knowledge that made my heart burn, for my sins were many and almost too much for me.

The next morning I was snowed under with work. Several

caravans had arrived simultaneously, and, as usual, everyone was in a hurry. Donkeys were braying, drivers were cursing, and owners were shouting for attention. The dust was so thick you could hardly see; the noise so great you could hardly hear.

As I glanced up from my records, I suddenly found myself looking into the face of Jesus. The same winsome smile was there—the same quiet, yet forceful sense of peace and power.

"Levi," He said, "Follow me." Then, turning His back, He began to walk away. Without a moment's hesitation, I rolled up my records, tossed my money bags to the Roman guard, and left everything to follow Him. To this day I have never once regretted my decision. For I was offered not only redemption for my sins, but a place in the believing community and an unbroken fellowship with Him through all eternity.

It was several years before I could understand how he could see an Apostle in a publican; or how He could have known the hidden hunger and the Divine desires that were camouflouged by a cursing tongue and a rough exterior.

But can you imagine what others must have thought? I heard Simon Peter muttering to himself that evening, "Oil and water just don't mix," while others of the disciples murmured just loud enough for me to hear: "We could have told the Master what sort of fellow this Levi is."

But I did not care, so great was my joy; nor did I blame them.

After all, it was as if your Community Chest had elected an embezzler for its chairman; or your Republican Party had nominated a communist for President; or the visiting Methodist Bishop had gone home to Sunday dinner with the local tavern keeper.

Jesus did go home to dinner with me that night and I invited all my wealthy friends to meet Him. It is still true that when a man meets the Christ, he is eager to introduce his friends to Him, and to share his experiences and his new way of life.

And it is still true that the outcasts of the world do not always live on skid row. Sometimes they live in three hundred thousand dollars houses and yet are outcasts from God.

That night at dinner the Master gave me a new name, just as He had done with Simon.

"You shall be called Matthew," he said, which means "the gift of God." I accepted my name gladly, for it signified more than a new name. It signified a changed life and a new relationship with God. Truly, it was God's gift.

And so I left everything behind in order to follow him. Well, not quite everything. I did bring along my pen and ink and my years of training in Rome's "Bureau of Internal Revenue." I brought along my sharp, "adding machine" mind and my observant eye; my instinctive regard for order and my business acumen; my ability to get the facts straight and to arrange them in precise detail.

All these I brought along and turned them over to the Christ. Thus it was that I became an author and wrote a book.

What talents have you turned over to Him? Or have you even answered His call? He may not want you to write a book, but He does want to make a new creature of you.

As you gather in grateful remembrance of His death and resurrection, what greater proof would you have of His Divine claim upon all of life than a publican, who by His grace, became a Saint?

I am Matthew, whose name means "gift of God." You, too, have received His gift. What are you doing with it

PHILIP

My name is Philip. I was born in Bethsaida on the north shore of the Sea of Galilee, near the mouth of the river Jordan. My father was a Jew, living in a Greek colony under the rule of the Romans. Bethsaida, which means "fish house" was at one time the slum area of nearby Capernaum. Philip, the Tetrarch, son of Herod the Great, was appointed ruler of this sparsely settled area in 4 B.C. by the Emperor Augustus, and within ten years he had made the Province a strong line of defense against the Parthians, with strategic lines of commerce and communication centered in our little city of Bethsaida, which soon became the prosperous capital city of the entire Province.

Near the end of that ten-year period, I was born, and my

61

father named me Philip. His orthodox friends muttered in their beards: "Why not Isaac, or Jacob, or David, or some other good Jewish name?" But my father was insistent, and I carried this Greek name the rest of my life.

But from my father I received more than a Greek name. Through him I learned the language of the Greeks and something of the traditions and philosophies of these strange people who had come from far across the seas. I learned to be receptive to new ideas and influences, and was not, therefore, caught in the web of strict orthodoxy that often closes the mind to new truth.

Oh, I remained a loyal Jew nevertheless, graduating with honors from the Synagogue School and with my classmates, Simon and Andrew, spending much time in religious debate about the future of our nation Israel. Along with them, I became a disciple of one John the Baptist, a great prophet and preacher, and was baptized by him in preparation for the coming of our Messiah.

One day John the Baptist preached a flaming sermon on the immorality of Herod the king. A great crowd followed him at the end of the service as he moved through the winding streets of our city toward the river Jordan. There a great number were baptized by the prophet, among them a strange young man about our age and dressed in the simple garb of a peasant.

Suddenly John flung his arms aloft and in a voice that could be heard far down the river he cried, "Behold the Lamb of God that taketh away the sins of the world!" We all stood transfixed, wondering what in the world was happening. Could this be the Messiah? But no, he was too young, too inexperienced, too plain a young man! In no way did he resemble our idea of a Messiah. Yet all the way home we talked about the incident, wondering what it meant.

The next six weeks were quiet ones for John the Baptist had been put in prison by King herod and there was not much activity among his disciples. But I had not forgotten the events at the river side, and I searched the ancient Scriptures in hopes of finding an answer. But no answer came.

Then one morning as I was walking along the sea shore, I saw a group of men coming toward me, deeply engrossed in conversation. I easily recognized Simon and Andrew, and as they came nearer, I recognized James and John, who often sailed on the Sea of Galilee with them, but the other figure I could not identify.

But as they drew near, I recognized the young man whom

John had baptized some weeks ago. He looked much older now. His face was deeply tanned from long exposure to the sun. His eyes had a strange power in them and His voice, though quiet and subdued, had a ring of authority.

For a moment I thought they would walk right by me. But then the young man turned, looked me full in the face, and said, "Philip, follow me."

And I did. I don't know why. I didn't even know His name or who He was. Perhaps I reasoned that if Simon and Andrew had joined forces with him, it would be all right for me to do so too. Perhaps I was still remembering that ringing cry of John the Baptist, "Behold the Lamb of God," or perhaps it was just that wonderful look and the note of authority in His voice that suggested in two words that my search for the Messiah was over. "Follow me," He said.

I did follow Him, and I learned who He was. The desire of the ages suddenly became a living experience for me as the creature shared with the Creator the timelessness of spiritual reality, discovering who I was, and to whom I really belonged.

I shall never know why Jesus singled me out to become a disciple. Simon and Andrew, and James and John searched for Him until they found Him. But Jesus searched for me. Perhaps it was His great love for ordinary people that He "saw into the depths of human souls, souls that appear to have no depth at all to careless eyes."

Or perhaps He saw in me some evidence and possibility of leadership because of my Greek background. Jesus must have known even then that the new wine of the Kingdom of God could not be contained solely in the old skins of Jewish legalism. So He welcomed me, Philip, whose very name indicated an appreciation of the wider world of men for whom the Christ would die.

As a member of the Twelve Disciples, I did not do anything dramatic. In fact, the first three Gospels do not even mention me except by name, but the fourth Gospel relates four incidents about me which may be of some help to you in your Christian life.

The first thing I did right after lunch that memorable day was to seek out my close friend Nathaniel. "We have found him," I shouted, "of whom Moses in the law and also the prophets wrote, Jesus of Nazareth, the son of Joseph."

"Huh!" Nathaniel grunted, "Can any good thing come out of

Nazareth?" But then Nathaniel had always been a skeptic, even as a young boy. I did not stop to argue with him—he was too clever with words and I would never have convinced him. I simply grabbed him by his tunic and said, "Come and see, come and see." And he came to meet the Christ.

Every band of disciples, even in your twentieth Century, needs those who desire above all else to share the Christ with others.

Every age, including yours, has its skeptics who love to argue religion. But argument often obscures. "Come and see," is the only answer. Have you invited anyone recently to meet Jesus Christ?

The second incident in my life took place just outside Bethsaida where five thousand people had gathered from near and far to hear Jesus preach and to participate in the miracles of His healing power.

The crowd began to grow restless in the early afternoon and Jesus realized that they were hungry. They had had no lunch. Turning to me He said, "Whence shall we buy bread that these may eat?"

It was natural for the Master to ask that question of me, for while Judas was then the treasurer of our band, it was my responsibility to find food and lodging as we travelled through Galilee. I had already been giving some thought to the problem and had done some quick calculation. There was no time to go all the way back to the city for food, there was little money in our treasury, one denarius, which was a working man's pay for one day, would buy only thirty six bitesized loaves of bread, two inches by an inch and a half. A year's pay would not buy enough to give this crowd one bite apiece.

"Master, we have only two hundred denarri," I replied, "and that won't buy food for five thousand people."

But with all my careful calculations, I had reckoned without Jesus Christ. I had been so busy finding excuses and reasons for not carrying out the Master's concern, that I had failed to see a young boy offer Him his lunch of five loaves and two fishes.

And when I turned to face the crowd, they were seated in orderly fashion on the ground and each had enough to eat. I am not sure whether it was simply a matter of each sharing what he had with another, or whether it was completely the Master's doing, but in any case, it only proved again how much He could do with so little.

You think your talents, your time, your money, your prayers, your worship mean little? To Him they mean everything!

The third incident was a brief one when a band of Greeks came seeking Jesus. Presuming, perhaps, that I was a Greek because of my name, they asked me to take them to Jesus. But I was not one who enjoyed the limelight, not one to push myself forward, and I did not like to have important decisions thrust upon me, so I turned them over to Andrew, and he took them to Jesus.

The Greeks saw more than they bargained for since it was near the end of the Lord's ministry and the inner struggle of His soul could now be seen. To these Greeks He said, "The hour has come for the Son of Man to be glorified..unless a grain of wheat falls into the earth and dies, it remains alone; but if it dies, it bears much fruit.

He who loves his life, loses it, and he who hates his life in this world will keep it for eternal life."

Here was revealed for us all the struggle of the will to live against the demands of self-sacrifice, the temporal against the timeless, the human against the Divine.

No words have ever been adequate to convey the meaning of Christ's cross, but in the presence of the Greeks we sensed the message of redeeming love and in the years to come we remembered these words.

At least "once to every man and nation comes the moment to decide." You can let the matter rest for awhile and reach a decision by way of no decision, you can argue the salient features of all religions, or you can kneel at the foot of a cross and accept in faith what God has done for you that you could never do for yourself.

The final incident took place in the Upper Room. Although we did not know it at the time, Jesus was delivering His final sermon to us. He was talking about God the Father and His great love for all men.

Almost without realizing what I was doing, I interrupted the Master, saying, "Lord, show us the Father and we shall be satisfied."

A breathless hush settled over the room and every eye was fixed on me. But it was too late. The impetuous question could not be withdrawn. But was it wrong to want to see the spiritual clothed in some physical form, to know clearly and precisely, to see directly and plainly, and to have spiritual truths expressed with the same definiteness as a sail on a ship, the fruit on a tree, or the cup on the Table before us? Was it wrong to want to see God?

Of course, I did not know what I was asking. I wanted scientific proof, a special miracle of some kind, a "clincher" to justify my faith.

With a look of infinite patience, the Master said to me, "Philip, have I been so long with you—in Cana at a wedding feast, on a hillside feeding five thousand, preaching in the synagogue, healing in the villages, restoring the sight of your blind friend in Bethsaida, raising Lazarus from the dead in Bethany, sharing all I know of the Father with you in the intimate hours of our fellowship—and yet hast thou not known me, Philip?

No man sees the Father, yet each act and word that expresses His will makes God known. Philip, can't you understand that you have been seeing the Father all along as you lived with me?

"He that hath seen me hath seen the Father."

And then turning to the others at the Table, He said, "I shall leave you soon. But when I have gone away from you, men hungry for God will come to you saying, "Show us the Father." Do the works that I do and thus reveal God to others as I have revealed Him to you. Truth is not a mystery to be understood, but a life to be lived. Truth is never understood until it is lived.

I am the truth, the way and the life. No man cometh unto the Father but by me."

Do you look for God, demanding a little extra proof for your own satisfaction before you can believe, as if a little private vision of some kind is your right, when God has already poured out His life for you on a Cross, and has raised up Christ from the dead?

What more can you ask? What more must He do? What more do you want?

NICODEMUS

My name is Nicodemus. In Greek the name means, "Victor over the people." As you might surmise, with a name like that I was descendant of a distinguished, aristocratic family.

One of my ancestors, in 63 B.C. was an ambassador to the Roman Emperor, Pompey. Even as in your day, ambassadors were usually wealthy people, and such was the case with my grandfather who served in the Emperor's court.

It was also true of my Father and his family who together controlled much wealth.

As a wealthy man, then, perhaps you think it a strange thing that I should have requested an interview with an intinerant carpenter known as Jesus of Nazareth. But it was not so strange when you consider my background.

My academic record in school was a good one and my parents wanted me to go into the legal profession, but I had always dreamed of serving in the synagogue. Happily, both professions were possible. I became a lawyer, but I also became a Pharisee, one of nearly six thousand in my day, whose sole duty it was to keep the laws of God. It was a momentous occasion when I took my oath of office in the presence of three witnesses, one of them my own father, and gave my sacred promise to spend the rest of my days in observing every detail of the law.

You of the twentieth Century are well aware that the Law of the Jews was contained in the first five Books of the Bible, known as the Pentateuch. But there were Scribes in our day who interpreted these laws for us and wrote many rules and regulations as to how we Pharisees were to observe them.

For instance, one law which also binds your conscience, was "Remember the Sabbath Day to keep it holy." But how was one to keep holy the Sabbath of the Lord God?

Well, our Scribes took care of that matter! They laid down many rules for the observance of the Sabbath—so many, in fact, that the "Mishnah" contained twenty four chapters of regulations; the Jerusalem "Talmud" had sixty four columns of rules; while the Babylonian "Talmud" contained one hundred and fifty six double pages of regulations.

You see, it was not easy to be a Pharisee, "A separated one" as the name implies, and you may well wonder why I, a Pharisee, sought an interview with Jesus of Nazareth who openly flaunted many of our laws.

It was also my distinguished honor to be one of the seventy members of the Sanhedrin, the Supreme Court of the Jews. There it was our duty, along with many other responsibilities, to examine and deal wisely with false prophets, in order that our religion might not be defiled by every strange creature who came along with a new idea about God.

Perhaps you will also think it strange that I, a Judge of the High Court, should seek out a self-styled prophet from lowly Nazareth in order to talk about my soul.

But I did request that interview. The many miracles and teachings of this strange Man kept mulling through my mind until it seemed I could not be content until I had met Him in person.

Recognizing my position as a leader, and letting my cautious nature rule my judgment, I requested that the interview should take place under the cover of darkness. Perhaps I was a coward, but it was something of a miracle that I could overcome my prejudices to meet with Him at all.

And yet, it was not too strange a request. For all the Rabbis of my day did their studying at night, believing, as some of your twentieth Century experts, that the best time for the pursuit of intellectual things is just before bedtime. Actually, I wanted the prophet all to myself, for there were so many questions I wanted to put to Him, and during the day He always seemed to be surrounded by great throngs of people where there could be no privacy.

Thus, through His disciples, the interview was granted and I spent the intervening hours rehearsing very carefully what I would say.

Then, almost before I knew it, we were seated together on a hillside overlooking the city of Jerusalem, with the night winds whispering through the trees and the sounds of the city echoing in the far distance.

"Rabbi," I began, "we know that you are a teacher come from God; for no man can do these signs unless God is with Him."

There was silence for several minutes and I wondered if He had heard me. Then He spoke:

"Truly, truly, I say unto you, unless a person is born again, born anew, born from above, he cannot ever see, or know, or be acquainted with, or experience the kingdom of God."

This was not the answer I had expected and now it was my turn to keep silence as I pondered what to say next. We were conversing in Greek, the language of the intellectuals of our day, and I was astonished that this country carpenter had such a grasp of our language. As in the Rabbinical Councils where Rabbis would debate at length the meaning of a single verb, He had just given me a complete interpretation of the Greek word.

Could this uneducated prophet have known that when a proselyte came into the Jewish faith, we Rabbis accepted him "like a new born child?" Indeed, many long hours were spent in discussion of this process. There were those who claimed that, theoretically at least, this meant one could marry his own sister, or even his own mother, because he was completely a new man. Old connections were severed once and for all. Now life was completely new.

So I thought: must I give up all my religious training and my strict observance of God's law to become as a "new born child" in this Kingdom of which He spoke?

But no, for He himself had said as much a few days earlier, while preaching to the crowd on the mountain top: "Think not that I am come to abolish the law and the prophets; I have not come to abolish them, but to fulfill them."

It was not to become as a "new born child" then, that was required by His teachings. I could keep my observance of the Law.

Could it mean, then, being born for the second time?

Since we were speaking Greek, obviously He was acquainted with the Mystery Religions of Greece, founded on the identity with a suffering, dying and rising God, where the object was to get the listener to identify himself so closely with this God, as to be in union with him, and thus, in the words of the Greeks, "twice born."

Several times I had seen the most famous of the Greek Passion

Plays in which the candidate was placed in a pit with a lattice over his head, on which a bull was slain, bathing the initiate in its blood. Thus the candidate came forth washed in blood, re-born for all eternity.

Perhaps this is what the prophet meant about being born again. So I asked finally: "How can a man be born when he is old?"

But again, He did not answer my question directly. Looking up into sycamore trees overhead, where the wind was still gently stirring the leaves, He said:

"It is unpredictable, mysterious, divine. It is like the wind— suddenly it is felt and then it is gone. You do not know from whence it came or where it went. But you felt the wind. So with the Spirit of God. So God breaks in upon a person's life."

He paused a few moments and then continued, as if I had understood his remarks perfectly thus far:

"You Jews are awaiting a Messiah," He went on, "Your ancient prophets have given you God's word that He will one day come to dwell with you in the Person of His Son."

I nodded my head in agreement. "And when that day comes," He said, "whoever believes in Him, trusts Him, clings to Him, relies on Him, will not perish but have eternal life. For God will not send His Son into the world to judge, reject, condemn or pass sentence on the world; that the world may find salvation through Him. And he who will believe in Him shall not be condemned. So it will be with everyone who is born of the Spirit."

It was not until months later that I came to understand how this new birth was not only being born from above, of God, but also meant becoming a "new born child" in Christ, a "twice born" man, if you please, and yes, washed in the blood of The Lamb.

But it was too much for me to grasp that night on the hillside under the trees, and I could only shake my head and ask, "How can this be?"

It wasn't that I did not understand my own need of re-birth; I had lived long enough to see evil at work in the world and in my own soul; but my intellect got in the way.

And because I could not understand HOW it works, I could not accept it just then. Standing within an inch of the Kingdom of God, I backed away into the darkness of the night.

It remained for a crucifixion and a resurrection from the dead to open my eyes to the power of God's Spirit let loose in the world.

I am not proud of the fact that I was so blind to the truth of

God that even laying His body in a tomb was like roses at a funeral—a gesture of apology for a friendship I might have claimed in life.

But I AM proud, and also very humble, in the knowledge that my interview with the Christ that night long ago provided the setting for the greatest text of the Bible, His last words to me, Nicodemus:

"For God so loved the world that He gave His only begotten Son, that whosoever believeth in Him might not perish, but have everlasting life. For God sent not His Son into the world to condemn the world, but that the world through Him might be saved."

Now, as I take my leave of you this morning, let me leave just one question with you:

"Are you satisfied with the condition of your soul?"

If people do not want to be re-born by the power of the Living God, they will deliberately misunderstand what it means to be born anew.

If people do not wish to be changed, they will deliberately shut their eyes and their minds and their hearts to the Power that can change them, saying:

"No thank you, I am quite satisfied with myself as I am, and don't want to be changed."

Then it will be easy to sit back and discuss the intellectual truths of Christianity without ever experiencing its power.

But let me remind you that the Christian faith is not something to be discussed; it is something to be experienced, to be lived.

When you people put yourselves in the hands of a physician, or when you undergo surgery, or are given some medicine to take, you do not need to know the anatomy of the human body, the scientific effect of the anaesthetic, or the way in which the drugs may work.

But you accept the cure that results without being able to say how it took place.

So in the realm of faith. There is a mystery still at its heart, but it is not the mystery of intellectual appreciation—rather it is the mystery of Redemption.

I know! For I am Nicodemus; not a murderer nor a criminal; not a pagan nor an atheist nor an outsider; but a living example of how the Holy Spirit can bring new birth even to those inside the Church.

71

This, then, is my story. May it make you more ready to welcome the promptings of the Holy Spirit, in knowledge that God can transform your frustrations into His marvelous success; that if we are faithful to small tasks of the moment, tremendous things may come to pass.

It could happen even in this place.

God, let it happen!

BARTIMAEUS

There once was a man who argued to himself that if he could push a button to ring a door bell, no more than pushing a button would be necessary to light a spotlight. So he simply transferred the wires, only to discover that it takes five hundred times as much power to light a spot light as to ring a doorbell.

How much easier it is to make a noise than to create a light. [1]

The Bible tells us that "in many and various ways God spoke of old to our fathers by the prophets, but in these last days He has spoken to us by a Son who reflects the glory of God and bears the very stamp of His nature." Jesus said, "I am the light of the world. He that follows me shall not walk in darkness, but shall have the light of life."

"As long as I am in the world," He said, "I am the Light of the world." [2]

On three different occasions Jesus healed men who were blind. To one He said simply, "Receive your sight." With another He simply touched his eyes. The third was told to go wash in a certain pool.

Would it not be an inspiration for us if we could actually talk to these men who were so healed of their blindness, to learn more about their condition before and after they met the Christ?

Well, let your imagination loose then, and imagine that one

72

of these blind men has returned from the First Century and now stands here in my place, speaking to you:

I am Bartimaeus, son of Timaeus. My father was a Greek, and like his father before him, a tradesman in the city of Jericho. In Greek, my father's name meant "one highly prized" and as his only son, I, too, was highly prized by my parents. What great dreams they had for me, dreams that included an education in Athens, dreams of my one day standing in the Forum as a leader of my people.

Then suddenly disaster struck. While playing soldier with a group of teenage boys in the neighborhood, I was struck blind by a wayward arrow, and all our dreams came crashing down upon us.

In the days that followed, like those of your generation, who are blind, I quickly developed muscular memory and obstacle sensation, which enabled me to move about rather freely. Through persistency there came a special sensitivity and keeness of ear, which enabled me to hear things I had never heard. But can you imagine what it meant to be blind? To be unable to distinguish even between day and night?

Then one day when my father and mother were on their way to Damascus to purchase goods, they were set upon by a band of marauding tribesmen and killed, leaving me alone in the world. It was the end of the world for me.

Oh, I tried to be brave. For a while I ran my father's business as best I could with the help of a neighbor, but it was difficult for me to bargain for things I could not see, and little by little the profits melted away.

It would seem that people are quick to help a blind man across the street, but equally quick to cheat him when a business opportunity arises.

Sure I was bitter. Who wouldn't be? I was too proud to ask for help from distant relatives and so I drifted here and there throughout the city, keeping body and soul alive through the generosity of friends. And then even that help was withdrawn.

So, I became a common beggar. What else could I have done? As one of your blind English poets once asked, so I murmured, "Doth God exact day-labor, light denied?"[3] Here I was, still in the prime of life, with nothing left to me but to beg. Such was my lot, such was my fate.

"Alms! Alms for the love of Allah," I would cry, as do the

beggars of your eastern world still today, learning to put just the right plaintive note in my voice in hope that I might secure some sympathy and a coin to exchange for bread. Thus I continued to eke out an existence, weary month after weary month, and weary year after weary year.

Now and then I would beg near the doors of the Temple, where I hoped people might be a little more generous. There I would hear references to a Messiah who was going to come some day to save His people; "to give light to them that sit in darkness." On one occasion I heard a preacher quote from the prophet Isaiah how God would some day,

"Bring the blind by a way they know not; lead them in paths they have not known; make darkness light before them, and crooked things straight."

"Hear ye, hear ye deaf," shouted the preacher, "look up ye blind that ye may see."[4]

But a lot of good it did me. How could you look up when there was no sight in your eyes?

One Sabbath, as the people were leaving the Temple, I heard a new excitement in their voices. They were talking about a new Prophet, one Jesus of Nazareth, who possessed miraculous powers and had actually healed two men who were blind. I learned that this Jesus was coming to Jericho soon and right there and then I determined that I would meet this man. After all, what did I have to lose? Maybe, maybe He really was the Messiah and would heal me.

Early in the morning of that memorable day, I established myself at the gate to the city, where customarily Benjamin the cripple did his begging. When Benjie appeared a bit later an argument ensued, but he had never before seen me so determined, so he hobbled off to another corner, mumbling threats about taking care of me later.

Soon I heard a crowd approaching. As the noise and confusion grew louder, I asked several people near me if Jesus of Nazareth was coming, but no one would even answer my question. Finally, a young lad brushed by me, close enough so that I could grasp his arm. Twisting it a little in my eagerness, I put my question to him. "Sure, it's Jesus," the boy said, and squirming out of my grasp ran off to join his friends.

Now I had prepared a little speech to give when I met Jesus, but what use was it now? No one could hear a word in all the din and clamor. But I had to do something.

Lifting my voice I shouted, "Jesus, son of David, have mercy on me."

As I have indicated, people are usually quick to help a blind man, because he can see neither the dangers nor the joys of life. And normally he commands some sympathy from individuals.

But not from a crowd. A crowd is undisciplined with charged emotions. Crowds are usually cruel and this one was no exception.

"Shut up Bartimacus," shouted a merchant down the street.

"Be off with you, beggar," said a well-dressed woman, gathering her skirts about her.

"Take your rags somewhere else."

"Who do you think you are?"

"Quiet, you fool."

These, and other angry rebukes, were quickly thrown at me.

Of course I knew that a beggar, and a blind beggar at that, was the lowest of all people. I had been told enough times that I occupied the bottom rung of the social ladder. So I had no right to claim the attention of this important man. I was just a street person.

But sometimes a man is desperate and here was the chance of a lifetime, slipping through my fingers. Half rising to my feet, I shouted even louder, "Jesus, son of David, have mercy on me."

Suddenly the noise of the crowd dropped to a whisper. Instinctively I cringed, imagining a Roman soldier striding toward me with upraised spear. Well, I had been beaten before, and, as I said, there was nothing to lose, save my life.

Then there came a quiet voice, saying, "Bring him to me." I could not tell from whence the voice came. Indeed, it seemed as if it could only have come from Heaven itself. But I needed no further encouragement. Leaping to my feet and casting my garment from me, I started toward the crowd. Mind you, I owned nothing in life, save that old ragged coat, but you can be sure that I did not stop to say, "Here, watch my coat." Sometimes there are things more important than the comfort of the physical body.

Assisted now by many willing hands, I was propelled forward until I sensed that I was standing before Jesus. Now there was not a sound anywhere, save the chirping of a cricket nearby and the soft lowing of cattle on a distant hill. The crowd was breathlessly expectant.

75

I ran my tongue over dry lips and was aware that my finger nails were biting into the palms of my hands. Here at last was my great opportunity. But you know what? I forgot my speech! Not a single word could I remember.

Then Jesus was speaking again. "What do you want me to do for you, Bartimaeus?" He said. His words caught me off guard. It was a little like telling a man he can have three wishes. If this prophet had the power that others claimed he had, if He was God, then there was nothing He could not do for me.

For a dizzy moment I thought of wealth and power and knowledge and social prestige—all the things that had been denied me from my youth. Then I said, "Lord, let me receive my sight." Now I was no longer a beggar seeking alms, but a sufferer seeking light. I knew I did not for a moment deserve what I had requested, yet I hoped He might at least do something for me.

"Receive your sight, your faith has made you well," He said.

For one stunned moment I stood there unable to speak or think. And then, as a fog lifts to reveal the glory of a sunrise, there came into my view the most glorious face I had ever seen! Deep set eyes looked into mine, plumbing the depths of my soul, with a compassion and love I never dreamed existed. Then He smiled, and laid a hand on my shoulder, and I was alive again, after all these years."

"I can see! I can see!" I shouted. And then I could not see enough, of trees, and skies, and people's faces, and my eyes fairly danced over the landscape of my beautiful Jericho, nestling there beneath the hills just as I had known it as a boy.

Strange, isn't it, how easy it is to lose sight of many important things in life without knowing that you have lost them?

Turning again to look at my benefactor and to speak my thanks, I found He was already moving on down the street where another crowd had gathered under a sycamore tree, in whose branches was hiding a little commissioner of taxes named Zacchaeus. Slowly I followed Jesus and the crowd, feeling my way with my cane from force of habit and forgetting that my eyes were no longer blind.

A few days later I followed Him into Jerusalem with a great multitude of people; and up to the Mount of Olives with a crowd of soldiers; and up a hill called Calvary with a crowd that had grown cruel again.

And I am still following Him. Once I was blind, but now I

can see that the Light of the world is Jesus. And I am still remembering the day when He performed His last miracle on earth, singling me out from the crowd to bring sight to my eyes and salvation to my soul.

As I leave you good people now, let me leave just one question with you. How good is your sight?

Oh, I know you can see things, but how well do you see the Christ? Is He blurred by your busyness, dimmed by your denial? Is He blotted from sight by your pride, or obscured by your prejudice? Is He obliterated by your obsession with things, or shrouded from your eyes by unforgiven sin? Do you really want to be healed of whatever blindness may be yours?

Here He calls to you, even as He called to me long ago in Jericho. Here as you surrender your wills to Him, as in my case, it may be no ordinary hour, but THE moment in your life.
I know it can be so, for I am Bartimaeus,
     who once sat alone beside the highway begging,
my eyes were blind, the light I could not see;
I clutched my rags and shivered in the shadows.
Then Jesus came and bade my darkness flee.

So people of your day can find the Saviour able.
Who can conquer passion, lust and sin?
When broken hearts have left them sad and lonely,
Then Jesus comes, and dwells Himself within."[5]

As one of the great preachers of my day put it, "But you are a chosen generation...that you should show forth the praise of Him who called you out of darkness into His marvelous light."[6]

I am Bartimaeus, beggar turned believer, a blind man who not only found his sight, but found the Light of the world.

ZACCHAEUS

I am Zacchaeus. Though I am mentioned in but one episode of your Holy Bible, you are well acquainted with me, for I am the little man who once climbed a tree in order to see Jesus.

But let me tell you about myself. I was born in Jericho some twenty years B.C. of a long line of Jewish merchants. My father was not only a wealthy distributor of the many fruits and vegetables grown in our lush valley, but also had a controlling interest in the largest industry of our city—that of making ink.

Jericho was a fabulous city, situated in the Jordan Valley just five miles above the Dead Sea. It's history goes back eight thousand years B.C. and many famous men have been citizens of Jericho.

From your Bible reading you know about some of them, such as Lot and Benjamin, Elija and Elisha, and Joshua, who fought a great battle at Jericho. Then, in my day, there was blind Bartimaeus, whom Jesus healed, and the Good Samaritan of that famous story, who did his duty to one who fell among thieves on the Jericho road.

From your study of history, you also know about Mark Anthony, who presented the city of Jericho to Cleopatra as a gift, as if it were a mere trifle for such a mistress.

You will also have read how King Herod the Great died in Jericho, with his last breath ordering the slaughter of many of my people, so that there would be someone to mourn when he died.

All around the city, which lay like an oasis eight hundred feet below the level of the sea, rich harvests were gathered each year of balsam and sycamore, bananas and grapes, and our famous roses which constantly perfumed the air. Truly my boyhood was

78

spent in one 'of the most beautiful cities of the world.

And it was a busy city. Day and night the streets were crowded with much activity. Pilgrims enroute to the Holy City could be seen rubbing shoulders with beggars and fanatics from the hill country, while Temple priests and rough soldiers mingled with rich merchants travelling the famous trade routes.

And legend has it that in the stillness of the early morning hours, now and then, "strains of temple music from Mount Moriah were borne along on the breeze of faint echoes, like the distant sound of many waters under the glorious summer sky."[1]

In such a wonderland and amidst such luxury, early in my youth I determined to get my share of the wealth that was everywhere evident in Jericho, and thus it was that I became the chief tax collector for the Roman Government. Where else could one make a better profit and with so little labor?

Sitting in the seat of customs day after day, I levied great taxes upon the balsam that passed through the market, still known in your day as "The Balm of Gilead." And there were great caravans of costly imports from Arabia and from Damascus that also yielded great income for my personal account.

And so I continued my attempt to amass a fortune and was doing right well, day after dreary day, laying my hands on wealth, but really seeking peace and dignity and self-respect.

When you think of bygone days, it is always interesting to note the epitaphs of famous men. For example, Moses was known as a lawgiver; David as a shepherd lad turned King; of Bartimaeus, whom all of us in Jericho knew, it was said, "And he was blind;" of Lazarus, "And he was a beggar;" of Naaman, "And he was a leper."

My epitaph was created long before my death and read: "And he was rich."

But to my neighbors and friends, I was classed with robbers and cutthroats, with adulterers and traitors.

Sooner or later, of course, a man must come to grips with his reputation. What people say about you is important, even if it is not always the truth. Even in your twentieth Century idle tongues can "hamstring a President, ruin an artist, hang an innocent victim of circumstances, unfrock a minister, or wreck a home. Bandying about careless estimates and idle verdicts may be appallingly serious. It may help to limit the sphere and narrow the horizons of someone's life."[2]

One day, when I had begun to think rather seriously about my standing in the community, a junior clerk came breathlessly to my desk with the news that Jesus of Nazareth had entered the city. I had been hearing much about this strange prophet, whom some claimed to be the Son of God, the long awaited Messiah. One of my close business friends, Matthew, had left his position with the government to become a disciple of this man. I was curious to know what kind of a person He was.

Quickly I closed my books, gave my staff the rest of the day off, locked my office and hastened down the street.

Already great crowds were gathering in front of the shops and markets where it was rumored He would pass. Moving in and out among the people, I sought a vantage point where I might see Him.

Suddenly the crowd began to cheer and a band of men drew near. But I could not see a thing! Even teenage boys blocked my view.

And to my surprise, the prophet was not being carried on men's shoulders, as one of His representatives of your twentieth Century is always carried, nor was he riding in an open chariot as important men of my day always rode. Apparently, He was walking in the midst of people.

Remember now, I was short of stature—just a little over five feet tall. The limitations of my body had plagued me all my life and had given me a kind of inferiority complex, I suppose, for which I compensated by robbing the rich and poor alike, when they came groveling to my tax office.

But I wanted desperately to see this man who had been so outspoken concerning publicans, of which I was chief; who had, on the other hand, once praised a repentant publican and condemned a proud Pharisee; who had publicly declared that it was nigh unto impossible for a rich man to enter the Kingdom of God.

And see Him I would! Just down the street was a large, spreading sycamore tree, typical of the many that lined our city streets. With experience born of many a youthful escapade, in a matter of seconds I was safely perched amid the friendly branches of that tree.

Now I could see Him as He walked slowly toward me, pausing now and then to speak to someone in the crowd or to lay a hand of blessing upon some child that clamored for His attention.

There was something about His countenance that at once both

attracted and disturbed me. What a strange man He was. Many thoughts of what our prophets had proclaimed concerning the Messiah were running through my mind, when suddenly He was beneath me. And, looking up into my face, He said, "Zacchaeus, come down."

Amidst the noise of the crowd and the din of the market place not far distant, that Voice seemed to thunder as from Mount Sinai, yet others around scarcely seemed to hear.

Of course, it was my imagination—or was it?—that seemed to say:
"Zacchaeus, come down from your lofty
perch in life. Humble yourself and
become even as these little children.

You have always been a climber. Now
your conscience is sick and your soul
discontented.

Come down out of your hiding place,
from the screening leaves of hesitancy,
come walk with me.

Climb down, Zacchaeus, and give your
climbing soul a chance."

Before I knew it, I was standing on the street, looking into that wonderful face.

Unconscious now of the crowd, I only knew that He had thrown an arm about my shoulder and we were walking along together—Saviour and profiteer.

Oh, I did not know Him yet as Saviour, though others had called Him Messiah. And I must admit that I was a little proud that He had singled me out for attention. It must have showed on my face, for Dr. Luke later wrote about my joy in his Book.

Nor did it bother me when the crowd began to murmur about the Master consorting with sinners. I was accustomed to hearing insults and had long ago steeled myself against such epithets.

Soon we reached my home and entered the luxuriant coolness of the house, leaving behind us the heat of the day and the heated words of the crowd.

While my servants were preparing dinner, we sat down to talk.

Since I was accustomed to defending myself because of my

occupation, I began at once to tell Him all about my parents, what God-fearing people they had been and how my grandfather had been a priest in the Temple.

But He did not say anything to that. He just looked at me.

So I told Him how from my youth I had kept the law of my fathers, giving a tenth of my wealth to the Temple.

But he did not say anything. He just looked at me.

So I spoke of recent gifts I had made to the Temple Building Fund and the contributions I had made from my business for the poor.

But still He did not say anything. He just looked at me.

And as His gaze burned into my very soul, making me feel naked and ashamed, further words of explanation died on my lips. And there was silence in the room.

I know not how long that silence lasted, for I was alone with my thoughts in the presence of One who seemed to know what I was thinking, and in whose presence my pretense and pride melted away.

And then at last He spoke. "The Son of Man is come to seek and to save the lost."

The lost?

Yes, as a city that is lost when rebels revolt, as a traveller is lost who misses the turn in the trail, as a sick man is lost when his disease is incurable, or a prisoner lost when sentence is passed upon him, so, in a moment, I knew that I was truly lost in the maze of life.

As I looked into those deep set eyes, my whole life was mirrored before me. And there was nothing of which I could be justly proud. There was no health in me.

Like many another man since, I cried: "Lord, what must I do to be saved?"

"Believe in me," He said.

"I am come that ye might have life, and have it more abundantly" than all the riches of the world can buy.

"I am come," He said, because "God so loved the world that He gave His only begotten Son, that whosoever believeth in Him might not perish but have everlasting life."

"I am come," he said, "that the world through me might be saved."

Suddenly I knew it was all true. Words cannot describe to you the peace and joy that swept over me as I knelt at His feet.

A rich man could enter the Kingdom of God when he learned to dedicate his wealth. And dedicate it I did, beginning first with those whom I had wronged.

Many months later I learned the full story of God's plan of salvation, but from the moment I knelt at his feet, it was true, just as He said, "Salvation had come to my house."

And what have I to say to you of the twentieth Century? Just this:

I once climbed a tree to see Jesus of Nazareth. And any man who sincerely wants to see the Christ will use every opportunity to break through difficulty and opposition to see Him.

I sought God, unknowingly, in groping discontent with my life.

But God sought me, knowingly, and found me in Jesus Christ. That encounter redeemed my past, transformed the present, and glorified the future. He can do as much for you!

For here the Lord of Life confronts you.

Here is visible evidence of the love of God for sinful people.

Here is mirrored for you what you have been and what, by the grace of God, you can be.

Not merely in the words you say,
Not only in your deeds confessed,
But in the most unconscious way
   Is Christ expressed.

And from your eyes He beckons me,
And from your heart His love is shed,
Till I lose sight of you—and see
   The Christ instead.

I am Zaccaeus who once climbed a tree. I am Christ's man. So can you belong to Him.

SERVANT OF THE HIGH PRIEST

There once was a man who stood on the Biblical stage but for a fraction of a minute and is mentioned by name in only the Gospel of John, although the event in which he plays a part is mentioned in all four Gospels. But because he is there, in the greatest publication of all times, he is worthy of our consideration.

So turn your imaginations loose for a moment and imagine that this man has returned from Judea to stand in my place here and speak to you:

I am not a preacher, not a disciple, not even a Christian. But I come to you of the twentieth Century with an inner hunger about which you know something. Let me tell you about myself.

I was born on the east side of Jerusalem only a few days after Jesus was born in nearby Bethlehem of Judea in the days of Herod, the king. My father was an alcoholic and my mother supported our family by scrubbing floors in the Temple. When I was just an infant, the edict of King Herod imperiled my life. But mother was equal to the situation and concealed me in the home of an uncle in Samaria until the danger passed. Other than this, my early years were uneventful, spent for the most part in the back streets of Jerusalem where I worked at odd jobs to help support our family.

Then, through friends of my mother, I, too, found employment in the Temple where I came to the attention of the High Priest and was eventually given a job as his personal servant.

My knowledge of the east side proved to be of great value to Caiaphas, the High Priest, and over a period of time I received several promotions. Eventually, I was allowed to sit in on the many important meetings of the Temple Council. What a revelation it was to be an inner part of the religious machinery,

84

presided over by my employer. And so the years passed.

Then one day Jesus of Nazareth appeared in Galilee, preaching a strange new doctrine. At each meeting of the Temple priests, more and more time was spent in discussing this new prophet. As his popularity grew, so did the concern of the religious leaders grow. Soon even I began to despise this Man, whom I had never seen or heard, because he was upsetting the smoothly functioning religion of the Temple and filling our people with strange notions about God.

But my curiosity was aroused, nevertheless. So, one afternoon, on my day off, I slipped out of the city to hear him preach in nearby Jericho. It was a long walk and when I arrived, there was such a crowd around him that I could not get near. But I heard Him clearly. What strange words He spoke:

"Whosoever would be first among you shall be servant of all," He said. "For verily the Son of man came not to be ministered unto, but to minister and to give His life a ransom for many. The Son of man is come to seek and to save that which was lost."

Never had I heard such words before! That night I lay awake for a long time turning over in my mind all that I heard and seen. Something seemed to have penetrated the very core of my rough being.

While I rejected His acceptance of Zacchaeus, whom we all knew to be a fraud, and was not sure that He had really healed the two blind men, still my heart longed to know more about this prophet. Was it true that I, a servant, could become first of all?

But during the busy week that followed, there was no further opportunity to hear Him again.

Soon all Jerusalem began to buzz with the news that Jesus had come into the Holy City. That night, an emergency meeting of the Council was called, which lasted until almost daybreak, and there we learned that one of the prophet's disciples was going to betray Him, so that Caiaphas could bring Him to the palace for questioning. Now I would see Him again!

But I could not wait. Something seemed to draw me out of my servant's quarters and I found myself following the palace Guard as it marched out in search of Jesus. As the lamps of the city dropped behind us, I grew bolder and actually joined the group of armed soldiers as they stumbled and cursed their way up the dark, dusty trail to Gethsemane. Soon we were in the

Garden.

By the light of the flickering torches, glittering against steel helmets and casting weird shadows around the olive trees, I saw a Man, robed in white, surrounded by a few shadowy figures. Unbidden, a warm glow came over me as I recognized Him. But before I could even move, a gruff order was given and the soldiers moved quickly to surround the little group of men. In the shuffle I found myself in the front rank, directly facing the calm and gentle Jesus. Almost unconsciously I moved forward a step to look again into that wonderful face, drawn by a power greater than mine own.

But hardly had I taken a step when I felt a searing pain shoot through the side of my face and felt blood streaming from the spot where, a moment before, my right ear had been.

Turning to meet my assailant, I saw the towering figure of a man whom we had come to know as the big Fisherman. Both rage and fear were written on his face and in his hand was a sword, from the tip of which dripped my blood.

Forgetting that I was but a servant, I tensed for further battle with this insolent fisherman, only to hear at my side a quiet voice, saying: "Peter, put up thy sword." At the sound of that wonderful voice I forgot my bleeding wound and turned again to look at Him. But already the soldiers were binding His arms and leading Him back down the rough Gethsemane trail.

Nursing my wounded feelings, and only half aware that somehow my right ear had been restored miraculously, I followed haltingly until we reached the palace courtyard once again.

Now I must admit that there I watched for a chance to get even with this Simon Peter. Oh, he was there all right, in the outer court, although he denied it when my cousin accused him of being one of the prophet's disciples.

However, for the next few hours, I was kept very busy by the Temple officers and sometime before dawn they took Jesus away to Pilate.

I never saw him again! But I have not given up my search for Him. They tell me He did not die but is alive forevermore.

My name is Malchus and here I stand in your twentieth Century with my dreams and longings unsatisfied. You may not recognize me, for I have changed my name and use many different names. I dress as you do, drive my own car, and am just a part of the crowd. But I am still seeking entrance into the circle of Christ's friends.

I am not a member of your church, and as far as I know I am not on any of your prospect lists. I am impressed by the superb organization of your churches and the good work you appear to be doing. Yet I remember the organized religion of my day, about which men and women were so concerned that they overlooked a servant in the house. In the midst of great Temple programs, somehow I, Malchus, missed the heart of religion which could have given meaning and purpose to my life.

Nor have I ever forgotten that Jesus of Nazareth did His best work with a few people.

So, here I am in your midst, still searching for Him. Who am I?

I deliver the daily newspaper to your door, service your automobile, harvest the wheat in your fields, babysit for your children, carry your clubs on the golf course, mow your lawns, shovel your walks, and perform many little services that you have come to take for granted while ignoring me.

Sometimes I am a teenager, searching for the meaning of life, finding none, save self-destruction.

And sometimes I work in the same office with your corporate executives, play bridge with you and your wives on occasion, share with you the Fund Raising for our Alma Mater and now and then make sizeable donations to your Church programs out of my wealth.

I admire the fine work you are doing and respect you for your accomplishments, but I am still searching for Him, who can give meaning to my life.

I am Malchus, the Malchus of the twentieth Century, nursing the scar on my ear, seeking admittance to the circle of Christ's friends, and pleading with you:

"Won't someone, please, introduce me to your Savior?"

PILATE

My name is Pontius Pilate. I lived in a drama-packed interval of history, although at the time it all seemed rather drab and monotonous. But let me tell you about myself.

I was born of wealthy parents in Rome, that great citadel of the earth at the very mention of which knees would bow and doors open. My early youth was uneventful, spent for the most part in the best schools that money could buy and in constant search of excitement and adventure.

Through my father's influence with the Senate, I was rapidly advanced through several political offices of government until one day there came the exciting news that I was to be made Governor of a Province, although I was still in my twenties.

Our whole family celebrated that night in great enthusiasm, but I could hardly wait to slip out and share the good news with Claudia, who was soon to be my wife.

In the midst of our marriage planning and all the happy excitement of those days, even the news that I would be sent to Palestine did not dim our joy.

But Palestine proved to be a very disappointing place. The wealth of our palace and the prestige of my office did not begin to compensate for the lack of friends and the social life we had come to love in Rome. Soon we came to dislike the Jews, who were always clamoring for something or other, and trying to get us into trouble with the Emperor.

Oh, I made some mistakes, as any young ruler would be apt to do. For instance, I thought I could get away with taking my wife along with me, although I knew it was like a Captain of a ship taking his wife on the bridge with him; but after all, we had just been married and I needed someone to share this important assignment with me. Besides, Claudia was of royal blood and knew how to get around the rules and regulations.

But someone did complain to Caesar and there was a mild diplomatic fracas, which eventually died down. But I hated the Jews

Nor did I anticipate their fury when I brought the Emperor's image into the city. What was one God, more or less, among so many? Apparently the Jews had different ideas.

For six days, seven thousand of them picketed my palace, praying to their Jehovah. And when I threatened them with massacre, it did no good. "It is better to die than to have images in Jerusalem," they cried. Knowing I could not massacre unarmed men, I had to give in, but I hated them for it just the same.

And then in arid Palestine water was always a problem, even as it is in your land every now and then. So, I decided to build an aqueduct to bring the cool waters from Solomon's Pool into the palace. It was a simple engineering problem, but as in your day, money was the problem.

Then I learned, quite accidentally, that there was a lush Temple Fund, created by taxing every adult Jew. It seemed expedient to use these funds to build the waterway—for the people. And so it was decided.

But what a clamor those Jews set up! Again they demonstrated for hours in front of my palace and even sending my soldiers among them, dressed in civilian clothes, did no good. And when some of them died, as a result, a complaint was sent to Rome. As a result, I got a scathing communique from Caesar, reminding me that it was my duty to keep peace in the land. So, my aqueduct never did get built and I hated those Jews.

Then there was one more incident you ought to know. My palace was everything that a Governor could desire, a place of splendor hard for you to imagine. Cascading waterfalls and beautiful formal gardens with fountains glimmering in the moonlight, made it a glorious oasis in the desert.

But I missed my Roman gods whom I had been taught to worship from childhood. So, I sent to Rome for the many shields on which my gods were pictured and set them up in the palace. But again the Jews complained and again an order from Caesar to remove them. How I hated those Jews!

Small wonder, then, that I was in no proper frame of mind when they came clamoring to my palace once again, this time at the unearthly hour of six o'clock in the morning. Now they wanted me to try one of their prisoners who had broken one of their thousands of laws.

"Tell them to come back 'at a decent hour," I thundered, only to be reminded by my counsel that there were some very important people out there—officials from other nations who had come for the Jewish Passover, and Caiaphas, the powerful high priest. All were insisting that I hear the case at once.

So I hastily washed and shaved and was anointed by my slave, and putting on my robes of office, I went down to the Judgment Place.

What a strange man faced me there! Amidst all the shouting and noise and confusion, he seemed to be the only calm person in the place. Obviously he was physically exhausted with great cuts and bruises on his face and shoulders, yet those deep-set eyes looked into mine with no fear or trembling. For a moment it seemed as if I were standing before him to be judged. From that first moment I knew that this man was no criminal.

"Take him and judge him yourself," I told the priests. "But it is not lawful for us to put any man to death," they replied.

Ah hah! So they had already judged him and found him guilty, had they? Well, it ought to be a simple matter to ratify their judgment and get back to the coolness of my palace. But something made me hesitate. I wanted to know more about this strange prophet out of Nazareth. So calling the priests to my side, I gave orders to withdraw into the Judgment Hall.

Facing the calm prisoner once again, I asked, "Are you a king, as these men claim? Is it true what these rebels say about you?" He did not answer my question, but began at once to talk about a kingdom that was not of this world and how he had come to bear witness to the truth.

Just another misguided fanatic, I thought, who will never learn that the only real kingdoms are those of armies and navies, of Emperors and kings..

"So you came to bear witness to truth," I said. "And what is truth?"

Knowing he could not answer that one, I did not wait for a reply but ordered the guards to take him out.

On the way to the palace balcony, I had a few moments to consider the strange fascination this man had for me. I knew he was innocent, even if he did think himself a king. But dare I risk my own neck to release him?

Reaching the balcony, I quieted the crowd which had gathered, and began to give my verdict: "I find the defendant not guilty," I said. But a great cry went up from the crowd, punctuated by angry shouts:

"He perverteth the people.

He would destroy our Temple.

He is a blasphemer.

Crucify him.

He stirreth up the people from Galilee

to this place."

Galilee? Galilee? So this man was a Galilean. Perhaps there was a way out after all. Calling the guards I ordered the prisoner delivered to Herod Antipas, Tetrach of Galilee. Let Herod deal with him.

Congratulating myself on my cleverness, I went back to my quarters with a relieved mind, absolved from an embarrassing situation.

But, as it turned out, King Herod was only interested in seeing some sleight-of-hand tricks performed by the prisoner who was supposed to possess magical powers. And when the prisoner would not even talk to Herod, he sent him back to me, now robed in a georgous many-colored garment.

So my strategy had failed. Here he was once again and I knew more than ever now that he was innocent and that I should set him free. It is always a judge's business to mete out justice, whether men throw mud and insults or cast compliments.

But the mob out there was on the verge of rioting now and something drastic had to be done.

But maybe there was still a way out. One of the Governor's many privileges was to release a prisoner to them at the time of their annual Passover. Reminding the crowd of this privilege, I asked if they wished Jesus of Nazareth released. Immediately a great shout went up, "Not this man, Barabbas."

Now Barabbas was a notorious killer, languishing in one of my prisons for his foul deeds. But what could you do with a blood-thirsty mob like that?

I released Barabbas, scoundrel that he was, and in spite of my wife's warning that this was a just man, in spite of my own better judgment, I decided to ratify the decision of the chief priests and sentence the prisoner to death on a cross.

Still, I made one last try. I gave orders to have the prisoner scourged, thinking that might suffice the crowd. Now you of the twentieth Century know little about this form of punishment, common to my day. But in some cases, even death was preferred than to be scourged by the whips of my Roman gladiators.

But even the sight of the prophet, with his red blood dripping on the white marble courtyard, did not satisfy the lust of the crowd. Now they would not even be quiet and I had to shout in order to be heard:

"Behold, I am bringing him out to you, that you may know that I find no crime in him. Behold the man!"

But they only cried the louder, "Crucify him. Crucify him."

And wily old Caiaphas, the high priest, moving like a snake through the great crowd, began directing a chant like an orchestra conductor synchronizes the voices of his instruments, and with one voice the people began to cry, "If you release him, you are not Caesar's friend..not Caesar's friend..Caesar's friend." And that did it!

As the words tumbled over and over in my mind, I realized that Tiberius Caesar was a hot-tempered, restless old man who would never listen to reason. Twice he had sent me a blistering communique—I could not afford another.

Calling the slaves for a basin of water, I washed my hands in full view of the vast crowd, and turned him over to be crucified.

But even these theatrics did not help. In my soul I did not even possess the courage to face my own guilt. And no matter how many times I washed my hands, light had turned to darkness, decency to deceit, justice to evil, and truth to villany.

Once my spirit gave a dying gasp later in the day when the noisy chief priests came again, this time wanting me to change the sign over the cross. "O wise Governor," they said, "make it read, 'He said he was king of the Jews.'"

"What I have written, I have written," I shouted. And how true it was. There was no turning back now. What was done, was done. It remained only to post a guard at the tomb and my Governor's seal on the great stone.

And what happened to Pilate after that, you ask? Oh, Tiberius Caesar ordered me home for trial and I was in prison a long time. Claudia stayed with the Christians in Jerusalem because she had come to believe in the prophet. Indeed, she is numbered "a saint" in some of your churches today.

But there was no hope for me. It matters not whether I died by my own hand as some claim, or was later beheaded by Nero, as others claim, for I had died long before my death.

Men do die like that, you know, and the greatest battles of history are fought on the field of men's souls. I know. For I am Pontius Pilate. Over the battlefield of my soul there is posted my epitath, which you yourselves have repeated hundreds of times:

"Suffered under Pontious Pilate," humanity's verdict concerning my deed.

And now as I take my leave of you, let me leave just one question with you:

What is your verdict concerning the Christ?

The Son of God is still being delivered into men's hands. God pity you if you leave your answer to the mob or someone else.

For each and all must eventually write their own verdict. However much you may worship, or debate, evade or postpone, a verdict must be rendered. Is your verdict this morning the one you wish to be your final one, when one day you will stand before him to receive his verdict concerning you?

Take my word for it, you of the twentieth century, strategy won't help. You can't expect someone else to make the decision for you, or to build your little part of the kingdom.

For he is delivered into your hands and you know who he is, that he is the Way, the Truth and the Life, Lord of lords and King of kings.

Nor will theatrics help you either, any more than they helped me. No matter how many times you wash your hands in the waters of procrastination, saying, "Not now, but when I'm not so busy; not now, but when I complete my education; not now, but when my career is established; not now, but when my social calendar is less crowded; not now, when I am young, but when I am old."

You can't wash away your decision—the Lord of life is in your hands. What will you do with the truth, with the Christ, your King?

What will your verdict be?

BARABBAS

It was a wise Creator who set us in families and systems, where we can know love and security, where we can grow and develop our potential, where we can relate to our fellow human beings, and where we can accomplish goals that no one of us could reach by ourselves.

These systems are sometimes religious, sometimes political. Some are educational or recreational, others philosophical or technological. Sometimes they are large systems, such as the United Nations; other times they are small, such as a village church set on a hill.

But we owe our existence, our growth and development, and our life work to these Institutional Systems that support and nurture us all our days.

However, in these days there are an increasing number of people who refuse to live in a system of any kind. These are impatient and unwilling to wait for systems to change, as change they must. So they take matters into their own hands, they take guns in hand and try to destroy the system by shooting a President, a Pope, or a Prime Minister, or by scattering pipe bombs around a metropolitan city to vent their anger.

Of course, this is nothing new, if you read history. Not too long ago young men goose-stepped across Europe to change the system into what they wanted it to be. They failed.

More recently in our own nation, young men raced up and down city streets, burning and looting in the riots of the 60's, to let the nation know that they would not live in the system anymore. To some degree, they succeeded. The system did change, somewhat.

More recently, thousands of angry young men have stormed

across your TV screens with clenched fists, determined to change the system in Iran. But you will probably be old men and women before this particular revolution has burned itself out.

So, you and I live in a violent world. Making peace may be the greatest challenge we will face in our lifetime. It will take a concerted effort and some systems may have to change, and we will be the ones to change them.

As Alfred Lord Tennyson put it in "In Memoriam":
"Our little system have their day,
    They have their day and cease to be;
They are but broken lights of Thee,
    And Thou, O Lord, art more than they.
Let knowledge grow from more to more,
    But more of reverence in us dwell."

During the American Revolution when our forefathers were rebelling against an unjust system, Voltaire wrote these words to Frederick the Great:

"It seems clear to me that God designed us to live in society— just as He has given the bees the honey; and as our social system could not subsist without the sense of justice and injustice, He has given us the power to acquire that sense."

Without a sense of justice, you see, we become very docile. This has been happening in America over the past fifteen years or so, as the American people seem to have fallen under a Pavlovian influence of some kind, reacting to terrorism and violent crime with an almost trained numbness. Some have become completely frustrated and have given up.

So, "to be or not to be" is no longer the question. The vital question is: "How to be, and how not to be."

During the Civil War, when still another system was undergoing change, Mark Hopkins, President of Williams College, declared in his innauguration address, "a student's mind is neither a piece of iron to be hammered into shape, nor a receptacle into which knowledge may be poured. Rather, the mind is a flame to be fed, an active being that must be strengthened to think and to feel, to dare, to do, and to suffer."

These words remind us that faith is not a noun, but a verb.

If faith were a noun, something you could define, hold in your hand, and pass around to others, then those bumper stickers of a year or two ago were accurate when they read: "I've found it." And other bumper stickers may have been just as accurate when

95

they read: "I never lost it." But the Church as one of those Institutions in our system, is not a lost and found department, for the simple reason that faith is who we are, and what we do in response to what God has done for us in Jesus Christ.

Faith is a verb.

E. Grady Brogue, Chancellor of LSU insists that "learning, loving, creating, serving—this is the faith of noble men."

Faith is a verb where we translate into action the deepest knowledge of God that we possess.

How will we live in a world of terror and violence? I'm not much of a sailor, having had all I wanted in the South Pacific during World War II, when yet another system was being challenged by free men, but I've always enjoyed the story of a young sailor on Long Island who was sailing his tiny boat from Plum gut to Montauk when he was suddenly caught in a thick fog. He was lost and a bit panicky.

Suddenly there loomed up before him a magnificent, mahogany-trimmed yacht. The young man shouted through the fog, "Which way to Block Island?" The yacht cut its engines and the experienced helmsman quickly laid his parallel ruler to his chart, and then shouted back through the fog, "East by south by half a south."

There was a moment of silence and then the young sailor called back, "Don't get technical, just point."

Let me see if I can point toward a solution for the problems which will face all of us in these troubled times. Turn your imaginations loose with me and imagine that a terrorist of the first Century has returned to the violence of the twentieth Century, and now stands here in my place speaking to you.

My name is Barabbas, which means, "son of a father." Which says nothing because every boy has a father. My first name was "Jesus," which means "The Lord is my salvation." This name is still common in your world, especially in Spanish countries, but since I looked elsewhere for my salvation, than to the Lord of life, your Gospel uses only my surname, Barabbas.

But let me tell you a little about myself.

I was born in the capital city of Jerusalem in the latter days of the reign of King Herod, the Great. My father was a stone mason and spent his entire lifetime working on the great Temple which Herod was re-building.

We lived a simple happy life in our humble home just a few

96

blocks from the Temple. Our pleasures were few and in the privacy of our home my father often cursed the Romans for their greed, but in public, like others, he was polite and obedient.

One night on his way home from work, my father stopped to listen to a political speech on the street corner, which soon developed into a minor riot that had to be quelled by Roman soldiers. It was over almost before it began, but three men were dead, one of them my father.

I was only a boy of fifteen, but from that day I swore that I would never rest until I had avenged my father's death.

During the next two decades, I spent every spare moment devising ways and means to harrass the enemy.

Other young men joined me and soon we had a revolution organized. It was not a full blown revolution, of course, and resembled more a dying campfire as the wind now and then fans the hot coals into flames. So our little insurrection would splutter and die, only to break out again as the winds of oppression fanned our zeal.

We thought nothing of stealing or robbing or even killing—it was all for the good of our nation. One night we waylaid a Roman sentry who was walking his post alone, and killed him. Moments later we were captured by a band of soldiers, who had set the trap to catch us.

The Roman Governor wasted no time in condemning us to death by crucifixion, but for some reason, perhaps because I was the leader and he wanted to make an example of me, I was detained in a dungeon cell for some time.

It was there that I began to hear rumors about another Jesus, a Galillean, who was also stirring up a revolution against Rome. We thought we had been unsuccessful, but apparently this Jesus of Nazareth really had the Romans up tight. The prison guards scarcely talked about anything else.

Then early one morning, the door of my cell swung open and I was ordered out. My ankle chains were removed and a dirty robe thrown around my shoulders to hide the hideous welts and bruises that were evidence of my daily beatings.

Moments later I was standing in the outer courtyard of Pilate's palace. There was a great, noisy crowd assembled there, including the High Priest and other important Jewish officials. Pilate sat on his portable throne, nervously wringing his hands and conferring constantly with his counsel. Something was up!

Then the Governor was speaking. I could hardly hear him, so great was the clamor of the crowd, but he was saying something about the innocence of the prisoner. At first I thought he was referring to me, although I knew I was not innocent of my crimes. But then my eyes became accustomed to the bright sunlight and I saw another prisoner standing before the Governor's throne. Dressed all in white, He stood quietly and obviously unafraid— the only calm person in the whole courtyard.

Once He turned to look at me, and those deep set eyes seemed to look right into my soul. I wanted to hide! Now I could look the strongest legionairre in the eye without trembling, and even the hiss and sting of their great whips could not bring a cry to my lips, but this was something else. It was the way my mother used to look at me with love and compassion as she ran her fingers through my tousled black hair.

But there was something more. Compassion and love was on that face, yes, but also a power; a power that seemed to caress my inner being and to awaken a response deep within me.

I turned away and moved a step behind my guard, so that I was shielded from that soul-searching gaze. No one could make Barabbas weep.

Suddenly, a great hush settled over the crowd and the Governor was speaking again, pointing at the calm prisoner and then pointing at me, he cried, "Which Jesus do you want me to release for you—Jesus Barabbas or Jesus who is called Christ?" Immediately a great cry went up from the crowd, "Barabbas, Barabbas."

Now doubtless you have never heard a great crowd of people shout your name in unison, unless you are a famous athlete of some kind, but let me tell you that it's a terrifying sound. I moved even further behind my guard, and for a moment considered making a dash for freedom, though I knew it would mean a spear in my back.

Hidden from the crowd, I was only half aware that a special detachment of gladiators, expert with the whip, was leading the other prisoner away. Shortly they returned with the prisoner arrayed in a bright purple robe and a make shift crown of thorns on his head. As his blood dripped to the pavement, the crowd became even more frenzied, demanding the death sentence from Pilate.

As I cowered there, still partially hidden from the crowd, I was only half aware that the Governor was making quite a show

98

of washing his hands in a basin of water. And I was totally unaware that my guard had removed the handcuffs and that I was unconsciously rubbing my chafed wrists and still blinking against the bright sun.

In a matter of moments, the entire courtyard was empty. Everyone, the Governor, the guards, the other prisoner, the people—had suddenly disappeared. I was alone, absolutely alone.

It was like a dream. You know the kind where you try to run away but cannot move.

There I was—a patriot, a revolutionist, a robber, a murderer, prepared to die on a cross for my crimes against the system, but miraculously set free by One who died on that cross for me.

I did not know what to make of it.

Do you know what to make of it?

I must leave you now, but as I go, let me leave just one question with you, Pilate's question: "Which Jesus will you have?"

Jesus Barabbas—the noisy one who appeals to the eye and the ear, or

Jesus the Christ—the quiet one who appeals to the conscience and the heart?

The Jesus who lived by the sword, or the Jesus who lives by love?

The Jesus who escaped death to laugh in the face of men, or the Jesus who died on my cross to save the world of men?

As you look down the decade that lies before you, you may be able to see a light at the end of the tunnel, but then again, it may only be the locomotive rushing at you. Because many, in the days ahead, will elect to follow Barabbas. Some will elect to follow the Christ. He's in your hands now. Which Jesus will you have?

JUDAS

I am Judas, disciple of the Christ. My reputation is such that you no longer give your sons my name, for it is commonly associated with deceit and betrayal. Even my friends of the First Century would speak my name like the hiss of a snake. "Judas-s-s Is-s-scariot," they would say.

But let me tell you about myself. I was born in Kerioth in the southern part of Judea, where my parents, though not wealthy, were leading citizens of the community. Like other boys I received my early education in the Temple School. Unlike other boys, my father had connections with important people which gave me the advantage of further education under the greatest professors of our day. Indeed, I was one of the best educated young men in the nation.

Perhaps it was because of my learning that I was so passionate for the cause of freedom. How I hated those Romans who treated us as if we were dirt under their feet; and how I dreamed of the day when we would be a free people.

Then one day I heard by the grapevine that there was a prophet in Nazareth proclaiming a new kind of kingdom. My heart pounded at this news and within a few days I was on my way north. Of course my father was disturbed for he had great plans for me in his business, and my mother shed hot tears at my leaving them alone in their old age. But I had to go. It was a long walk, about seventy miles, but at last I found the prophet and was invited to join his band of men. Eleven others had already been chosen, all of them Galileans, which perhaps accounted for their unwillingness to accept me for a time. But when Jesus made me the business manager for the group, entrusting me to work out the schedule of appointments and handle the finances, the others reluctantly admitted me to full membership.

What dreams I had for the future! But how quickly I was disappointed. Here was One who could speak and the blind would see; could gesture with His hand and the lame would walk; who could but lift his little finger and the angry waves would subside; or lift His voice in prayer and raise the dead. Yet, He frittered away His time in Galilee, talking to beggars and prostitutes and tax collectors. Many a time, as I tossed on my bed at night, I would ask, "Why doesn't He get a move on? Why doesn't He sweep Rome into the sea and establish His kingdom now?"

As I look back from this vantage point, I can see that I was possessed of a narrow, intolerant, nationalistic spirit—a kind of perverted patriotism. Oh, my Lord was a patriot, too, but with a far great vision of the kingdom of God which would one day include all people.

But I could not wait. And my impatience expressed itself on many an occasion. For instance, we were visiting in Bethany when Mary lavished much costly ointment on Jesus and I could not hold my tongue to remind Jesus of how much good the money could have done for the poor. But my Lord, from the look He gave me, must have known that I was really thinking of what that money could do in setting up our Kingdom.

And, of course, I was interested in advancement. It was only natural for me to desire a chief place in the kingdom which I had served long and faithfully. I was not alone in this desire. Peter once asked Jesus, "What reward shall we have?" But always the Master put us off, vaguely referring to His Kingdom as "not of this world." And so the days dragged on and the kingdom was no nearer than when we first banded together.

But the people were excited and the chief priests were greatly disturbed by the things which were happening. Thus, when they approached me secretly one night, without thinking I agreed to force the issue by placing Jesus in their hands.

It was the time of the Passover Feast and Jesus had sent Peter and John ahead to find a banquet room. They would find a young man carrying a pitcher of water who would take them to the banquet hall. Jesus and the other disciples walked the two miles from Bethany in the hot afternoon sun and arrived at the hall where stood the traditional water jar and towels, ready for use.

It was a common practice of that time to remove one's sandals and wash the dust and grime from the feet, assisting one another

101

in the rinsing and drying process. But not that night! Each disciple stalked by the water jar and towels to sit down at the Table without washing. It is easy to imagine that even our faces betrayed our inner feelings of anger and sullenness. Oh, we were not angry with Jesus, but with each other and with ourselves.

Earlier on the road that afternoon James and John had tried to claim the best seats in the Kingdom. Now James and John had always been a bit uppity, being a cut above the rest of us socially, and by virtue of their blood relationship to Jesus. But the other disciples were angry with James and John for having tried to get ahead of them. And we were no doubt angry with ourselves because we had not thought of the idea in the first place. So, we were in no mood to wash one another's feet.

This disturbed Jesus, of course, and He probably wondered if three years of teaching had been for naught. Were His disciples willing to love each other in general, but not in particular; to love the world, but not the one sitting next to them at the Table?

How could the Master teach us now? Well, He could say to Peter, or James, or John, or even to Judas, "Wash my feet," and we would have obeyed in the twinkling of an eye. Jesus could have said, "Wash each other's feet," and again we would have obeyed instantly. But if we had missed His fundamental teaching of three long years, one more command would probably not suffice. No, something more dramatic, more astonishing, was needed at that moment—something that would trouble our conscience and jog our memory in the days and years ahead.

So, Jesus took a towel and girded Himself with it, and gave us not a sermon nor a lecture, not a command nor a scolding, but a parable acted out in a visible way. He washed our feet! And none of us ever forgot it.

As disciples of the Christ, you, too, often gather at His Table. Sometimes you may come desiring the chief seats in the Kingdom of God, places of honor. You, too, may not serve one another or serve for the sake of another.

Why should you teach other people's children so they can lie a bed on Sunday mornings? Why should you give up every Thursday evening and every Sunday morning, sometimes twice, for Choir rehearsal and worship, while others with equally good voices stay home and watch television? Why should you give the time to be church officers, or ushers, or circle leaders, or anything else, when others around you are even more talented and have more spare time?

It becomes a bit difficult to answer such questions, doesn't it? Especially when you see the Christ on His knees washing the feet of His disciples. And all He said was, "I have given you an example."

As I look back upon those hours of what you call "Holy Week," I am not sure of my emotions or my motives. I really thought He was our Messiah and therefore no real harm could come to Him. I really felt that it was time to force His hand and bring the Kingdom to pass. Believe me, it was not the money. What was fourteen dollars—the price to redeem a slave? If I had wanted money, I could have taken it out of the treasury and no one would have known.

What is the motive to betray one whom he loves? Never did I dream what would happen. There wasn't the faintest warning of the remorse I would soon feel. Nor was I prepared for the living hell into which my soul would be plunged.

"If hell were just the invention of palefaced theologians, long ago the race would have cast the idea overboard. But it still remains because it is not the invention of men who write books and uphold systems of thought, but rather the deep affirmation of the human heart. Remorse is the ground swell of the ocean after a storm. The storm subsides. The sky is blue. The air is balmy. There is not a white cap to be seen. But the ship heaves and tosses because of the mighty swell that remains.

So remorse heaves the soul as the tide the ocean."[1] No one has ever lived, I suppose, even the most thoughtful and tender, who did not regret, when a loved one was gone, some lack of ministry, something done or left undone, and who would not have given his all to have the dead back, even for a moment.

Let me remind you that I was not a monster, but a man just as human as you are. People have always been prone to consider those who go wrong as different from other people. But it is not so.

Possibilities of evil go hand in hand with possibilities for good. When the Master told us that one of us would betray Him, no one pointed a finger at me, or at Peter, but each asked, "Is it I, Lord?"

Jesus once told us that "he who is without sin, let him cast the first stone." And it is still true that only those who see in themselves the possibilities of sin can become the channels of grace to others. You should remember, therefore, that Jesus washed my feet, too. And He invited me to sit next to Him at the table so that I was the first disciple to receive from His hand the sop of unleavened bread dipped in wine. I was not a monster nor was there much difference between Peter and me. Each of us betrayed the Master that night. Each was a traitor.

But Peter repented. Judas did not. I had only remorse. I could not repent. So one lived, one died.

Of course, you have never deliberately plotted to hurt your Lord, now have you? But you, too, have your pride and your selfish moments. You, too, blurt out impetuous words and to impetuous things, now don't you? Then you, too, know something of remorse. In my remorse, I said, "I have sinned in that I have betrayed innocent blood," and I went to the priests to give back the money. But they would not take it back. So I hurled the silver coins upon the Temple floor in anger and can still hear the raucous laughter of the chief priests, and hear the ringing echoes of those coins thundering in my ears as they remind me of the verdict of all humanity concerning my deed.

But before you point the finger of scorn at me, as others have done through the centuries, let me leave you with a few questions.

Have you never resisted the pleadings of a loving mother; the earnest preaching of a good minister; the faithful instruction of a dedicated Church school teacher? Have you never stood silent while others profanely abused the name of your Lord? Have you adored Him in public only to push Him aside in the private practice of your life? Or have you never treated another human being as dirt under your feet or insisted that they "know their place," meaning a station in life and that is something less than that befitting a child of God? What is the price of your betrayal? Pride? Greed? Money? Power?

You are fortunate people indeed, for there is grace and help for you whenever you come to the Table of the Lord,. a Table that stretches twenty five thousand miles around your world—a Table that gathers disciples of every language, race, nation and class—a Table where Christ is always present. How I wish that I might join you. But remorse for what I once did still keeps me away. My epitath still reads: "One who might have been."

I am Judas, seeking forgetfulness in suicide, when there was mercy at the cross. It was there waiting for me. It still waits for you.

104

SIMON OF CYRENE

My name is Simon. Not Simon Peter, the big fisherman, not Simon Iscariot, father of Judas, not Simon, brother of Jesus who later headed the Church in Jerusalem, not Simon the zealot, nor Simon the leper, nor Simon the tanner, but still another Simon.

My name in Greek meant "pugnosed," but because I was born and raised in Cyrene, I came to be known as Simon the Cyrenian.

With the exception of a few years abroad in school, I lived all my early life in the capitol city of Libya on the beautiful southern shores of the Mediterranean. Built in 650 B.C. Cyrene was the center of a prosperous agricultural industry, a center of democracy since the year 400 B.C. and a Roman Province of note.

As a Jew I felt very much at home in this lovely city, not only because I could read and write Greek and Latin, but because Cyrene, along with Alexandria, was the center of a Jewish population of more than a million people there on the northern coast of what you call Africa. But like every Jew, my citizenship may have been in a foreign land, but my heart was in Jerusalem.

Although we had occupied this land ever since the Dispersion centuries before, and though few of us had ever visited the Holy City, yet we continued to pay the half shekel tax each year for the support of the Temple in Jerusalem, and to offer our daily prayers for her welfare.

Quite suddenly one day there came the opportunity to make a business trip to the city of my fathers. Fortunately it was the time of the annual Passover celebration and I found myself in the company of many other pilgrims enroute to the Holy City.

And what a thrill it was to stand at last on the hillside and look down upon the city of my ancestors. It was even more glorious than I had imagined. A lump came into my throat and my eyes were moist. It was like coming home.

As I stood there taking in the view of all that my eyes could encompass, I never dreamed that I would shortly play a walk-on part in the greatest drama of all ages. No other man would ever journey to Jerusalem to perform such a task, or to meet such a procession coming out of the city gates.

As a tourist, bent on seeing the Holy City, in all of its grandeur, I was happy and carefree going my own way, minding my own business and carrying no burdens. Then out of the blue my plans were completely changed. This does happen to most people at some time or other in their lives and I know you can sympathize with me. Few of you today follow trails on which you set out in your youth. Many of you have gone far afield, perhaps wisely, perhaps unwisely.

Making my way down in the city on that particular day, I was met by a noisy procession coming up the hill. Here and there could be seen the glint of the noon day sun reflected from the gleaming helmets of Roman soldiers who were apparently leading three convicts out to the place of execution. Carefully, I stepped aside to let them pass. But just as the three criminals, staggering under their crosses, came abreast, one of them stumbled and fell. Suddenly a rough voice gave me an order, "You there, give the man a hand."

At first I did not realize that the soldier was addressing me. I felt compassion for the one who obviously was so weak that he could scarcely walk, let alone carry the heavy cross beam. But it was none of my business. I was simply a tourist.

Then a heavy hand was laid on my shoulder and a voice shouted, "Come on, get going," and I realized that the soldier was talking to me. Pulling myself up to my full height, I was about to remind the soldier that I was a University graduate and a prominent business man in a Roman Province, but the point of a spear in my back made me hesitate.

Then, without so much as "by your leave," I was thrust forward into that maelstrom of shouting people, rudely, reluctantly, resentfully, and bent to pick up the cross beam. But first I turned to look closely at the prisoner. Blood was streaming down the side of his temple from a cruel crown of thorns that someone had jammed down on his head. His back was bruised with many a cruel welt that spoke of the stinging lash in the hand of an expert. The muscles of his arms and shoulders were glistening with sweat and he was gasping for breath.

My first reaction was one of anger. I knew that the Roman soldier who had commandeered my service could never have ordered another Roman to carry that cross, even as I knew that no Jew would so much as lay a finger on it. But obviously I was a foreigner so he conscripted me into service.

At first I was very angry with myself. "If you hadn't been so curious to see what was going on, you wouldn't have been caught up in this predicament," I muttered. And then my anger reached out toward the man whose cross I was bearing. Anger, of course, is seldom reasonable. Often we refer to it as getting mad. It really is a kind of madness and as I looked at the prophet, there must have been a measure of madness in my soul. If you couldn't bear your own cross, why did you ever allow yourself to get into a situation like this, I thought.

Suddenly the sting of a lash across my shoulders rudely interrupted my reverie, rough hands laid the cross beam over my shoulders and I followed the procession up the street from whence I had just come. Angry against Rome, angry with myself, angry at the prisoner whose cross I was compelled to carry, angry at the whole world, I stalked off to Calvary.

Not only had my plans been drastically changed and my life headed off in another direction, but now I had a burden on my back that was not my own.

Have you ever carried burdens that were not your own? Do you fret and chafe under them? Remember, then, that it is not what life does to you, but how you react to it, that makes all the difference in the world. Wrong reactions can change one's wealth into want, strength into weakness, blessing into curse.

Then the prisoner turned and looked at me. Never shall I forget that look. There was a light in those eyes that must have come from heaven—certainly from a heart of peace and love. For a moment I stood transfixed, seeing in that face something I never expected to see in my lifetime and which defied description.

There were few words exchanged between us but a kind of spiritual communication took place as he held me in his glance. The fires of anger in my soul were quenched and a great change came over me. I sensed a feeling of perfect peace such as I had never known before.

Now the heavy cross lay like a shepherd's staff upon me and I walked erect, carrying it with ease as if in a trance, while those strange words of the ancient prophet echoed across the centuries: "Surely he hath borne our griefs and carried our sorrows. He was wounded for our transgressions and was bruised for our iniquities. The chastisement of our peace was upon him and with his stripes we are healed."

A fleeting thought crossed my mind that this might be the way our Messiah would one day come. But no. No! This was no way to treat God.

Well, you know the rest of the story, the events that transpired in those next three hours until death was a welcome relief. If I were to describe them to you in intimate detail, it might be more than your gentle minds and hearts could take.

Certainly it was a day ear-marked for tragedy, an hour in which the most pitiful roll call in history took place: On the one hand devout priests and people answering, "Crucify him," while his friends kept silence; and on the other hand, just one affirmative voice, that of Pilate testing the wind with his finger to see which way it was blowing and then rendering his verdict "not guilty" only to change it again and cast his voice in the negative. At every point along the line, defeat. And at every point, victory!

I know. For I am Simon of Cyrene, the only man who ever carried on his back the actual wooden cross. No other man ever stood so near the wounded Savior. No other man was ever part of that last earthly conversation with the Lord. And I was there when they nailed him to the tree. I was there when they laid him in the tomb.

This then is my story. Thus it was that I became involved, quite unintentionally, in the greatest drama of history. Later that day I headed for home. There was no spark of desire within me to see more of the Holy City.

Several weeks later the great news arrived in Cyrene that He was alive. Death could not hold Him, for He really was the Son of God, even as the centurion had blurted out at the cross. I guess I had known it all along for in some mysterious way I had been led to sell my lucrative business and to sever all my ties in Cyrene. I was preparing for another venture of some kind, the details of which I did not yet know. And then came further news and another trip to Jerusalem and the experience of Pentecost and a place of leadership in the early Church. What a thrill it was to be one of the five who laid hands on the Apostle Paul to send him forth in mission for Jesus Christ.

It will not seem strange to you that my sons Rufus and Alexander also became followers of the Christ and were chiefly responsible for the Church in Rome, without which you might never have heard the Gospel.

As I take my leave of you now, let me leave you three things that I learned in my Christian experience.

First, I learned that everyone needs to learn how to carry burdens. In traveling about your wonderful country, it appears to me that the slogan of your twentieth Century might well be, "Give me security or give me death." And your common prayer, if you are honest, might be, "Lord, make us comfortable. Keep us safe. Make the job last. Keep wages high and the collateral sure, and let us live a long time, even if we do not live it well."

But a man or woman cannot live a sterile, antiseptic, withdrawn life. It isn't life, and it isn't living, when all around you there are people with pressing problems and deep hurts, carrying tremendous burdens; people who need love and concern rather than a flippant word or casual nod.

When the Lord of life was dying on a cross, He was thinking in love even of the tough customers beneath his cross, who were bawling and brawling in an alcoholic haze with no conception of what was happening right before them. But He was grieving for their souls. "Father, forgive them for they know not what they do." Is there any greater discovery than the discovery that someone cares about you? And that He does not reject you even though He sees through you utterly?

Once this miracle dawns on you, once you have grasped its truth, then love begins to stir in your heart and you learn to shoulder the burdens of others.

The second thing I learned was how to live with suffering. Jesus said, "In the world you shall have tribulation." He was not talking only about bodily disease and pains, but was referring to tribulation that comes when a disciple must stand for something in which the world does not believe. "If any man will come after me, let him deny himself, take up his cross and follow me." There it is in plain, blunt language. We are not only to know about the cross, but to know the cross. And you do not carry a cross without suffering. I know! Remember I carried one once, literally, and further than I was compelled to carry it. And I carried it for the rest of my life.

Of course Cyrenians are hard to find, even in the twentieth

Century. Do you never say, "Careful now, this may lead to suffering?" Are you never indifferent to spiritual things, especially when you have a bad cold; or willing to stay inside where it's warm when it's cold outside, even though it is the hour for worship? Does not your devotion trickle away when your feet are cold? And do you not get cold feet when your Christian principles are at odds with your friends of the world?

Wherever two divergent ways meet, a cross is formed. And if you have no cross. this simply means that your way parallels the way of the world. Friedrich Nietzsche, the intellectual father of Nazism which spawned so much hatred into your generation, once said of the anemic Christians of his day, "How little you know of life, you smug and comfortable people."

Calvary's cross was erected against a backdrop of greed and lust for power, of bigotry, pride, hypocrisy and hate, which has not yet disappeared from the world. To confront it in faith may mean suffering in a day when people all over the world are paying with their bodies for the desire of their souls. What one does with suffering, then, makes all the difference in the world.

Man, who takes full credit for most of the good things in the world promptly labels any disaster an Act of God. Some rebel against it. Some meet it with stoic fortitude. Some accept it as punishment. Others use it for the discipline of their souls. Jesus transformed it into love and revealed the character of God.

By His grace you can do the same, and thus, "you will know Him and the power of His resurrection and the fellowship of His sufferings."

The third thing I learned was to keep the cross in view. We early Christians represented many different nations, different languages, different traditions, different organizations and different beliefs. The Galatians were fickle, the Romans haughty, the Phillippians warm hearted, the Thessalonians irresponsible. And yet we were bound together into a living Body by a cross and a living Lord. Oh, we had our divisiveness, especially in matters of the creeds, but we were always one when we knelt in reverence beneath a cross.

It is good that you come regularly to the Lord's table beneath His cross, for some Christians of your day prefer the "Old rugged cross on a hill far away"—just as far away as they can put it in thought and imagination. Some have reduced the Christian faith to a cult that promises comfort without a cross. They sing, "Hide me, O my Savior, hide, till the storms of life are passed."

But when you sing, as you often do, "When I survey the wondrous cross on which the Prince of glory died, my richest gain I count but loss and pour contempt on all my pride," then you will not need to worry about your differences for you are not far from the Kingdom of God.

As I leave you now, perhaps I should remind you of one other thing. It was Christ's body that failed beneath the burden of the cross, but not His spirit. It is even so in your day. It is His Body, the Church, which sometimes fails, but not the spirit of the living Christ. His Body exists in the world because the Spirit is deathless and divine.

I know! For I am Simon of Cyrene who once carried the cross for the Christ. And O yes, I almost forgot to tell you, I am a black man. But then I do not need to remind you good people that the ground at the foot of the cross is always level.

FOOTNOTES

ZECHARIAH
[1] *Service for Company Publications*

MARY
This meditation can easily be dramatized by Tableau scenes on either side of a Chancel or Stage with costumed people illustrating the reading, as indicated by footnotes:

[1] Mary and the Angel
[2] Joseph in his shop
[3] Mary and Elizabeth
[4] Joseph in his room

[5] Mary and Joseph
[6] Manger scene with shepherds
[7] Manger scene with Wisemen
[8] Lighted cross

HEROD
[1] "For the Time Being: A Christmas Oratorio," from W.H. Auden: COLLECTED POEMS, by W.H. Auden, edited by Edward Mendelson. Random House Inc. Used with permission.

JOHN THE BAPTIST
[1] Adapted from the Liturgy of Malabar, fifth Century.

ANDREW
[1] *Prelude, Book 13*, Wordsworth
[2] *The Holy Grail*, Tennyson
[3] Gerald K. O'Neill, Princeton University Futurist Professor in *U.S. News and World Report.*

NICODEMUS
Scripture quotations from *The Amplified New Testament*, Zondervan Publishing House, Grand Rapid, Michigan.
The Lockman Foundation, 1954, 1958

BARTIMAEUS
[1] *Interpreter's Bible.*
[2] *Hebrews* 1; *John* 8; *John* 9.
[3] John Milton, *On His Blindness*
[4] *Isaiah* 42.
[5] adapted from *Then Jesus Came*, Oswald Smith
[6] *I Peter* 2:9.

ZACCHAEUS
[1] Alfred Edercheim, *The Life and Times of Jesus the Messiah*, Longman, Green Co., 1896.
[2] *International Bible*, Vol. 8.

SERVANT OF THE HIGH PRIEST
Delivered to the one hundred and sixty eighth General Assembly of the United Presbyterian Church USA Philadelphia, Pensylvania.
Published by *Pulpit Digest*, 1957. Used with permission.

JUDAS
[1] McCartney, *Great Nights of the Bible.*

112